THE
NEW AGE
RAGE

THE

NEW
AGE

RAGE

BY KAREN HOYT
AND THE SPIRITUAL COUNTERFEITS PROJECT

Edited by Karen Hoyt and J. Isamu Yamamoto

Power Books

Fleming H. Revell Company
Old Tappan, New Jersey

Library of Congress Cataloging-in-Publication Data

The New age rage / Karen C. Hoyt and the Spiritual Counterfeits Project : edited by Karen C. Hoyt and J. Isamu Yamamoto.
    p. cm.
Bibliography: p.
ISBN 0-8007-5257-0
1. New Age movement—Controversial literature. 2. Cults—Controversial literature. I. Hoyt, Karen C. II. Yamamoto, J. Isamu. III. Spiritual Counterfeits Project.
BP605.N48N48   1987
291—dc19
                                        87-19825
                                        CIP

CONTRIBUTORS

Frances S. Adeney is an instructor at New College, Berkeley. For two years she served as research director for Spiritual Counterfeits Project. She has an M.A. from the University of Wisconsin and is a Ph.D. candidate at Graduate Theological Union, Berkeley.

Brooks Alexander is cofounder and senior researcher for Spiritual Counterfeits Project. He is also the author of numerous articles on cults and world systems.

Robert J. L. Burrows received his B.A. from the University of Toronto and a Master of Christian Studies degree from Regent College, Vancouver, B.C. Before becoming a Christian, Mr. Burrows studied and was committed to the beliefs and practices of Eastern mysticism, particularly Buddhism. In 1975, after five weeks at Swiss L'Abri, the Christian community founded by the late Francis Schaeffer, Mr. Burrows committed his life to Christ. He is currently editor of publications and a researcher for Spiritual Counterfeits Project. Along with articles written for SCP publications, Mr. Burrows's work has appeared in *Christianity Today, Eternity, Evangelical Newsletter, Update,* and other periodicals.

Douglas R. Groothuis is associated with Evangelical Ministries to New Religions and is research associate with Probe Center Northwest, Seattle, Washington. He holds an M.A. in philosophy from the University of Wisconsin and is the author of *Unmasking the New Age* (Inter-Varsity, 1986).

Contributors

Dean C. Halverson is World Religions Specialist with International Students, Inc., in Colorado Springs. He holds an M.Div. degree from Denver Seminary. He has done research for SCP for several years.

Karen C. Hoyt is executive director of Spiritual Counterfeits Project. She has an M.A. in clinical psychology and works as a therapist in the San Francisco Bay area.

Art Lindsley is scholar in residence at the C. S. Lewis Institute in Washington, D.C., and a member of the SCP board of directors. He holds a M.Div. from Pittsburgh Theological Seminary and a Ph.D. from the University of Pittsburgh.

Paul C. Reisser is a physician engaging in family practice in Thousand Oaks, California. With his wife and John Weldon, he is a coauthor of *The Holistic Healers* (Inter-Varsity, 1983). He holds his M.D. from the UCLA School of Medicine.

Spiritual Counterfeits Project, under whose auspices this book has been written and edited, is a Christian, nonprofit corporation established to research and provide information on new religious movements.

Its basic purposes are:

1. To *understand* the significance of the spiritual turmoil and religious pluralism in our culture.
2. To *research* the effects and influence of the new religions, particularly those based on Eastern philosophies.
3. To *provide* a biblical perspective on the new significant religions and other movements so that the Church can respond appropriately.
4. To *produce* well-researched and accurate resources.
5. To *bring* the good news of Jesus Christ to individuals and society.

For more information about Spiritual Counterfeits Project, you may write directly to P.O. Box 4308, Berkeley, CA 94704, or call ACCESS/SCP HOTLINE, (415) 540-5767.

Karen C. Hoyt
Executive Director

CONTENTS

Contents

Part III: Wheat or Tares—Assessment

Part IV: Reaping the Harvest—Antidote

INTRODUCTION
Karen C. Hoyt

Is the New Age movement an ominous conspiracy, a new religion, a self-help movement, or just a passing fad? Is the New Age movement really of any significance? Does it have any impact on us? The New Age movement (NAM) influences can be seen in America's shifting religious beliefs. Currently, 23 percent of Americans believe in reincarnation; 23 percent believe in astrology; and 25 percent believe in a nonpersonal energy or life force. These beliefs are not compatible with Christianity and seem to indicate a growing trend toward a belief in the New Age religion.

The purpose of this book is to explore the many faces of the New Age movement thoroughly and carefully and to see how the New Age movement has influenced many areas of our lives, including science, health, medicine, psychology, and politics. In addition, there is an important overview of the whole movement and a chapter that deals with NAM's occult roots in India. Another chapter answers the question, "Is the New Age movement a global conspiracy?"

In the final section of the book, the authors discuss how to understand and give a loving Christian witness to those in the New Age movement. The book ends with a discussion of the meaning of Christian transformation.

In NAM, as well as in all movements, there is both error and truth. This book covers what we believe to be error in detail, but I would also like to say a word about the "truth" in NAM. NAM has brought to our attention important issues that we as

11

Christians have lost sight of or have undervalued. These are issues where there can be some agreement with NAM:

1. An emphasis on cooperation instead of competition (in a personal, not economic sense).
2. Protection of the creation, instead of exploitation and destruction of the earth's resources.
3. Creativity—Christians often find themselves defending mediocrity and rigidity, instead of encouraging spontaneity and creativity.
4. Promoting the cause of peace in the world.
5. Calling for radical transformation, a total change of mind even though our idea of the needed change is very different from NAM's.
6. The importance of the body and its care: exercise, healthy food, and so on.
7. Human potential and positive self-image—people are created in God's image—Christians support human potential and a positive self-image, but not *unlimited* human potential and not an unflawed self.
8. The global village—one of the most radical changes in the last twenty years is that we can no longer function as an isolated nation, politically or economically—a crisis in one country affects the whole world.
9. Working for a nontoxic environment.
10. Networking—when New Agers talk about this, some Christians get nervous and visualize world conspiracy, but the truth of the matter is that the most powerful and effective network ever is the Christian Church.

These are just a few of the areas in which Christians might agree with NAM, but on the deeper issues, there is profound disagreement and concern. Here at Spiritual Counterfeits Project we receive hundreds of calls and letters each year from concerned friends, loved ones, and associates of those who have converted to the New Age movement. This has sparked

SCP into continual and broad research in the New Age movement and its various ramifications.

What you hold in your hands is the cooperative effort of SCP and other experts in the area. I would like to thank the many contributors who have made this book a reality: Frances Adeney, Brooks Alexander, Robert Burrows, Dean Halverson, Douglas Groothuis, Art Lindsley, and Paul Reisser. We have followed the flowering of the New Age movement over the last thirteen years, and we are glad to offer the completion of this text as the fruits of our efforts.

PART ONE

PLANTING THE SEED— SEED— ANTECEDENT

1

THE COMING OF THE NEW AGE

Robert J. L. Burrows

LESS THAN A DECADE AGO, MENTION OF THE NEW AGE MOVEMENT WOULD have drawn blank stares from non-Christian and Christian alike. But all that has changed. In the 1980s, the term *New Age* is common currency, even if variously understood.

In the Christian community, awareness of the New Age movement has been triggered by a few apocalyptic speculators who have singled it out as the primary catalyst for the ultimate end. Coverage in the secular media has, up until now, been slight.

But recently there has been a flurry of attention, much of it sparked by Shirley MacLaine's five-hour TV miniseries, *Out on a Limb*. The series was a dramatic enactment of Shirley's spiritual search and amounted to what can aptly be described as an occult catechism. In the course of that five hours, the audience was introduced to reincarnation, telepathy, auras, out-of-body and near-death experiences, spirit channeling, candle meditation, and extraterrestrial revelation and guidance. The connection between this potpourri of esoterica may have previously escaped the general populace, but Shirley brought it

17

all together. If she communicated anything, it was that all of these seemingly disparate things point to a single conclusion: Humanity is divine and immortal.

Media attention and MacLaine's popularity may fade, but the New Age movement is no passing fad. It is firmly entrenched and deeply rooted—the outcome of an ongoing process that began in earnest during the countercultural era of the 1960s. During that decade, a sizable segment of American youth turned for inspiration to the vast and varied traditions of Eastern mysticism and Western occultism.[1] In that milieu and from those traditions, the diverse and diffuse phenomenon now known as the New Age movement (NAM) emerged.

The term *New Age* suggested itself because of the millennial gloss of many of the traditions drawn upon. The term was also seemingly confirmed by that most ancient of esoteric disciplines, astrology, which predicted a move into the Aquarian age at the close of the century. The very nature of the counterculture—its size and radical disaffection with the cultural mainstream—reinforced the sense that something novel and revolutionary was underway. And that sense of imminent transformation, conceived as the culmination of humanity's evolution, remains a hallmark of New Age enthusiasm to the present day.

---

[1] Definitions: *Mysticism* in its more popular sense is distinguished by (1) the affirmation of unity between humanity and deity; (2) the primacy of experiential knowledge; and (3) emotional ecstasy. If the first affirmation is denied, it is possible to speak of Christian mysticism—an intimate relationship with a personal God, experientially confirmed, marked by exuberant joy. The term *mysticism*, therefore, is not always used to denote religions that assert humanity's divinity, but that is the sense it is used throughout this chapter.

Occultism, popularly, is associated with Satanism or practices often dubbed "black magic." It is in other words used to refer to religious practices that have a sinister and evil intent. But throughout this chapter the term is used in a much broader sense. The root meaning of occult is "hidden." "Western occultism" refers to religious traditions in the West that suggest ultimate reality is hidden from ordinary perception. The beliefs and practices of those traditions profess to disclose ultimate reality's hidden truths.

Monism refers to those religious and philosophical traditions that affirm there is only a single reality in the cosmos. Derived from the Greek *monos*, meaning "one," it affirms "all is one."

The swamis and gurus of the radical sixties have largely disappeared, and "hippiedom" is now only a topic of nostalgic conversation. But that flush of mystical excitement is still very much with us, though it has taken new forms.

But mysticism's resurgence since the sixties has largely been one of secularization. The counterculture sheared its locks, picked up its briefcase, and moved into the cultural mainstream. "The ancient wisdom," as it has been called, made a similar transition. It has been largely shorn of its overt spiritual overtones and assimilated into the culture in secularized forms. In the decades since the sixties, theories, therapies, and practices based on the root premises of the ancient wisdom have proliferated, and the scope of application has widened to include every major facet of contemporary culture: science, business, health, education, psychology, religion, politics, the arts, and entertainment.

Because of its diffuse nature, it is difficult to estimate the number aligned with the New Age movement and even more difficult to assess its influence. Marilyn Ferguson, whose 1980 *The Aquarian Conspiracy* catapulted her into the New Age limelight, cites a 1978 Gallup poll that indicated ten million Americans were engaged in some aspect of Eastern mysticism (Ferguson 1980).

The Christian film *Gods of the New Age* arrived at a figure of sixty million through a poll that suggested twenty-three percent of Americans believe in reincarnation.

Whether espoused by ten or sixty million, the New Age worldview has emerged as a viable contender to both secular humanism and the Judeo-Christian tradition. Whatever the exact figure, its influence is far greater than its numbers.

What has emerged is a multifaceted, multifocused movement that is in many ways sociologically analogous to the evangelical community. Like evangelicalism, the New Age movement is not tied to any particular organization; has no overarching hierarchical structure; is diverse in both practice and belief; and though it has prominent spokesmen, it has no official leadership. What unites the New Age movement and links it to the traditions that preceded it are a set of common worldview assumptions about God (or ultimate reality), humanity, and the nature of the human predicament. Those assumptions, foundational to monistic and pantheistic traditions, have been designated by a variety of terms: *ancient wisdom, perennial philosophy, occult philosophy.* However designated, they can be summarized in the following three points:

Ultimate reality. In spite of the teeming diversity of the cosmos, reality is single. Ultimate reality—or God—is pure, undifferentiated energy, consciousness, or life force. This reality manifests itself in creation as the dynamic interaction of polarities: light/dark, male/female, aggressiveness/passivity, good/evil, and so forth. Those polarities, however, are not absolute. They are different facets of that single reality from which all creation emanates and in which all creation is united. In spite of appearances, all is one.

Humanity. Humanity, like the rest of creation, is an extension of God (or ultimate reality) and shares its nature and essential being. That divine essence is humanity's true, higher, or real self.

Humanity's predicament. Because there is no discontinuity between humanity and God, at any point, alienation caused by sinful rebellion is not humanity's fundamental problem. Metaphysical ignorance is humanity's snare. What divides us is a divided mind, blind to the essential unity of all that is and to humanity's innate divinity.

That blindness, the root of all humanity's woes, is dispelled by *gnosis*—experiential knowledge of the one and of humanity's essential deity. That knowledge is brought about by psychospiritual techniques which involve balancing polarities, manipulating energy, and ridding consciousness of the fragmenting effects of reason and the predefining limitations of belief. Only then is the unity of reality fully experienced; only then can humanity's divinity fully unfold. That is the path to godhood, self-realization, cosmic consciousness, *samadhi*, enlightenment, and—in our day—New Age transformation.

Though differing in expression, emphases, or implications

drawn, the alternative-reality traditions of Western culture that served as the forerunners to the New Age movement share the worldview summarized by those three points. To understand the New Age movement, it is important to have some sense of its historical predecessors. Occultism and Eastern mysticism in the West reach back as far as one cares to go. For the present purposes, the nineteenth century will do.

Historical Predecessors of the New Age Movement

Transcendentalism. In the early 1800s, English translations of Oriental scriptures made their way to the American public. Oriental thought became more accessible to the shapers of American culture, particularly the bohemian fringe of literary men and women, artists, and philosophers. The transcendentalists of the early nineteenth century stand out in this respect. Henry David Thoreau and Ralph Waldo Emerson, transcendentalism's leading lights, were wooed by the wisdom of the East. They represent a typical phenomenon, for in their hands, in some respects, the East did not remain the East. They were quite eclectic, borrowing what suited them and rejecting what didn't, filtering everything through the American ethos of self-determination and individual autonomy. In that important sense, they were the prototype of those who now form the New Age movement.

Spiritualism. The 1800s also witnessed the birth of two popular alternative-reality traditions, Spiritualism and New Thought. If a date for the former were to be fixed, it would be March 31, 1848, when the Fox sisters heard rappings allegedly communicated by the spirit of a murdered peddler whose body lay somewhere beneath their Hydesville, New York, house.

The rappings at Hydesville marked the birth of Spiritualism, that branch of occultism that sought to confirm the reality of the unseen world, and humanity's immortality, by communicating with departed spirits. That interest in reality's other dimensions broadened to include psychic or paranormal phenomena:

the ability to read minds, travel out of the body, bend spoons with thought, stomp over burning coals, and so forth.

The influence of Spiritualism led to the formation of organizations for the scientific investigation of the psychic and the paranormal. It was not, however, simply an inquisitive scientific spirit that inspired the Spiritualists' investigations. The phenomena under scrutiny excited the Spiritualists because they were seen as salvific signs, like the outpouring of the Spirit in the New Testament. But for the Spiritualists, these signs did not point to God's intervention to save those who were helpless to save themselves. For them, they pointed to humanity's innate capacities for re-creation, placing the possibility of fashioning the new man into humanity's own hands.

New Thought. The eighteenth-century Neoplatonist Emanuel Swedenborg (1688–1772) supplied the Spiritualists with the framework for their theories. From the Austrian physician Franz Anton Mesmer (1734–1815), the movement adopted the tools of trance. Mesmer was a key player in the nineteenth-century occult renaissance, influencing both Spiritualism and New Thought. Mesmer, who gave us the word *mesmerism*, was the grandfather of hypnotism. He used trance-induction techniques in his practice and suggested healing could be effected in trance states because of a current of energy, which he called "animal magnetism," that passed from healer to patient.

The American psychic healer Phineas Quimby modified Mesmer's explanation, proposing that it was not animal magnetism that healed, but the powers of the mind. Quimby's views were to find fervent support in the founder of Christian Science, Mary Baker Eddy, and would lead to the formation of numerous mind-science organizations: the Unity School of Christianity and the Church of Religious Science, to name but two. The New Thought movement continues to exert its influence. Much of the power-of-positive thinking movement can be traced to it, and the priestess of prosperity, Terry Cole-Whittaker, comes directly from the New Thought tradition.

New Thought's emphasis on the mind's power rests on the premise that all that exists is the Mind of God, which is in the

22

mind of men. If Descartes could say "I think, therefore, I am," the New Thought tradition, with equal conviction, says "I think, therefore, it is." From that affirmation, it naturally follows that mental orientation produces an individual's circumstances. Poverty is a state of mind and prosperity only a "right thought" away. That is why Terry Cole-Whittaker can unabashedly say, "You can have exactly what you want, when you want it, all the time" (Cole-Whittaker 1983, 3).

Theosophy. That affirmation could easily have been uttered by Madame Helena Petrovna Blavatsky (1831–1891), the founder of another strain of occultism that emerged in the nineteenth century. Blavatsky, an eccentric Russian noblewoman, arrived in America at the height of the Spiritualist excitement. Initially a Spiritualist supporter, she soon broke with the movement and, with Colonel Henry Steel Olcott (1832–1907), formed the Theosophical Society in 1875. Blavatsky and Olcott soon felt the tug of the East and moved to Adyar, India, soaking up all they could of the Hindu and Buddhist traditions that surrounded them. That exposure would have a marked influence on Blavatsky's extremely esoteric and elaborate writings, which were a dizzy blend of Western occultism and Eastern mysticism.

To those who followed in her footsteps, Blavatsky would pass on some seminal ideas. In line with Spiritualism, Blavatsky was also interested in communicating with those on the other side. But her spirits were not simply those of the departed; they were ascended masters, highly evolved beings who had moved up the spiritual hierarchical ladder and now supervened in human affairs, dispensing knowledge and power to the worthy. Blavatsky also waxed abstrusely on the idea of a spiritual evolution of the species that paralleled biological evolution, but that idea was not her invention.

Before the ink was dry on Darwin's *The Origin of the Species*, occult circles had appropriated the theory for their own ends. Evolutionary theory resonated perfectly with the notion of gradual progress that was implicit in the emanationist cosmology of occultists and mystics, seeming to put the authority of science behind what they had always believed. For if humanity had become human by passing through apehood, it seemed plausible enough that it was headed toward godhood. The permutations on that evolutionary theme were virtually endless and could be relatively innocuous or downright sinister. As history would show, it was just as possible to believe evolution applied to a particular race as it was to believe it applied to an entire species.

Blavatsky, for her part, divided human evolution into seven stages and believed a new phase and new age were on the horizon. It was at such times that the ascended masters would reincarnate as world teachers, to help humanity up the evolutionary spiral. Annie Besant (1847–1933), Blavatsky's successor, would take up that theme and supply the movement with a messiah. Besant, in collaboration with C. W. Leadbeater, founded the Order of the Star in 1911 to promote the young Indian Jiddu Krishnamurti as the avatar of the dawning new order. In 1929, however, Krishnamurti repudiated his messianic status and denounced the movement. The Order of the Star dissolved, and Annie Besant's Theosophical Society was never again the same. Messianic enthusiasm, however, is difficult to dispel, whatever form it happens to take. Blavatsky's particular version was resuscitated by her American devotee Alice Bailey in the first half of this century and by the British esoterist Benjamin Creme in the present decade. In 1982 Creme ran full-page ads predicting the reappearance of Lord Maitreya, the Christ. The year has passed and Creme, like so many prognosticators of the millennium, has been forced to revise his scenario.

In the larger picture, Blavatsky's messianic ruminations are but a drop in a sea of millennial speculation that has continued unabated since the first century. Her utopian vision may be unique in many of its details, but it illustrates two typical points: the commonly held view that each age has its avatar, and the equally prevalent view that Jesus of Nazareth was simply the avatar of His age. And that last point raises another: Western occultism and Oriental religions universally reject Christianity, but they frequently assimilate its terminology and its founder. Needless to say, the terminology is invariably infused with meaning foreign to its biblical sense, and Jesus is presented as a guru who dispensed nuggets of hidden wisdom directing humanity to the god within.

Theosophy certainly has done its share of dispensing misinformation about the Christian tradition. But, unfortunately, it is not alone in that regard. In the same era, Nicolas Notovitch popularized the myth about Jesus visiting the East during His so-called "lost years," where He allegedly studied under some Oriental adepts and returned with the message of monism. But Notovitch's myth was just that: a fantasy. Even the eminent orientalist F. Max Muller denounced the work as pure fabrication (Goodspead 1956). But it is a tenacious myth, still very much in circulation, constantly revised and revived.

Psychoanalysis. Another strand of note that would serve as a channel for the ancient wisdom was psychoanalysis, a new discipline that arrived at the close of the nineteenth century. In its infancy, psychoanalysis required pioneer thinkers to formulate theories about the inner workings of the human psyche. These inner realms had already been exhaustively explored by occultists and mystics, so it is not surprising that Sigmund Freud (1856–1939) and Carl Jung (1875–1961) were acquainted with occult literature and influenced by it.

Freud's antireligious sentiments are common knowledge. It goes without saying that the ideas he adopted were secularized and given a materialistic interpretation. But the occult revival's influence can be clearly seen in his initial adoption of hypnotism as a therapeutic tool. Unlike Mesmer, Freud did not attribute inherent healing properties to trance states, but like a medium conjuring ghosts from the underworld, he used trance induction to ferret out haunting repressions from the subconscious. Like the occultists, he assumed that ordinary states of mind were not the most reliable sources of truth.

In the main, Freud was successful in wresting borrowed concepts from the mystics' grasp by attaching them to inviolable instincts—particularly sexual instincts.

Freud's foremost disciple, Carl Jung, did not share his mentor's anxiety about the occult, mysticism, and magic. Jung was beset by paranormal experiences all his life and was an avid advocate of the alternative-reality tradition. He attributed one of his seminal works, *The Seven Sermons to the Dead*, to automatic authorship—ghostwriting in the most literal sense. It was, in fact, that dictation that gave Jung the basic framework for his psychologizing.

The points of contact between Jung and the occult are numerous. His "collective unconsciousness" echoes the mystical conception of the cosmos as mind. His idea that both good and evil are intrinsic to the self, which unites them, reflects the mystical notion that duality is intrinsic to the cosmos, which is ultimately one. Jung, like Freud, was also intent on giving his ideas a measure of scientific respectability. He was not, however, driven to provide everything with a materialistic explanation. As a result, Jung's psychology, far more than Freud's, represents a "restatement of the ideas at the core of occult tradition in terms accessible to those ill at ease with religious language" (Webb 1976, 387).

Oriental traditions. Oriental traditions certainly influenced all of these avenues, but they would not launch a major offensive themselves until the sixties. A number of earlier figures, however, paved the way.

The first missionaries from the East arrived on Western shores to attend conferences hosted by liberal Christians. Swami Vivekananda (1862–1902) left a favorable and lasting impression on the World Parliament of Religions held in 1893 at the Chicago World's Fair. Vivekananda, a pupil of the renowned Indian guru Sri Ramakrishna, stayed behind and formed the Vedanta Society. At the beginning of this century, the great Sufi master Hazrat Inayat Khan brought the teachings of his ancient lineage to the West. Paramahansa Yogananda arrived in 1920 to attend the International Congress of Religious Liberals, and went on to establish the Self-Realization Fellowship. And the silent, self-avowed avatar Meher Baba came to the United States in the early 1930s, adding his voice to the ancient wisdom's refrain: "Philosophers, atheists and others may affirm or refute the existence of God, but as long as they do not deny the existence of their own being they continue to testify to their belief in God—for I tell you, with divine authority, that God is Existence, eternal and infinite. He is EVERYTHING" (Baba 1976, 13).

Such were the historical predecessors of the New Age movement. All, in varying degrees, contributed to the counterculture's quest for an alternative to the spiritless secularism of Western culture. But the period that gave birth to the NAM supplied it with its most formative influences.

The Formative Decade: 1960–1970

Oriental traditions continued. Zen Buddhism was the inspirational focus of the fifties' beats, the final movement of major significance before the sixties' explosion. To the disenchanted Westerner, Zen had much appeal. Like Buddhism in general, Zen was a religion that wasn't a religion—in the sense that it was unconcerned, even agnostic, about the existence of deities. It was thus perfectly suited for the secular psyche. Zen embodied an implicit critique of the vain busyness of Western culture, because it was in essence a critique of the vanity of life itself—the futility of all desire and striving that in the end must come to nought. Zen was sassy; it was cynical; it was simple with a simplicity that verged on the simpleminded. "Eat when hungry, sleep when tired." That admonition captures the Zen spirit that cut through the complexities of the contemporary world, the hype and hustle of modern life, recapturing the exhilaration of living fully in the moment. For the disenfranchised beats of the fifties, who looked at the past in dismay and the future in despair, the ecstasy of the moment was a seductive philosophy, indeed.

The dismay and despair of the sixties' counterculture that followed was no less acute. The hippie generation found the mystical vision it embraced in that bohemian fringe and occult underground already in place. The widespread use of consciousness-altering drugs, particularly LSD, was a major

27

mode of initiation into that subculture, which became a mass movement. From the beginning, the psychedelic experience was tied to the enlightened consciousness of the mystics by its major propagandists, Timothy Leary and Richard Alpert. Alpert eventually became disenchanted with the ephemeral effects of drug-induced enlightenment and set out on more traditional paths to permanent bliss. He went to India, came back a changed man with a changed name, and as Ram Dass, became one of the more engaging and effective popularizers of the mystical vision.

Like Ram Dass, many others would make the trek to the Orient, but for those who stayed behind, India would come to them. In the 1960s and early 1970s, gurus from the East inundated North American shores. With the help of the media, these exotic visitors successfully dispensed the message of humanity's godhood and popularized the techniques traditionally used for achieving it: meditation and Yoga.

One of the first gurus to arrive, and certainly the most influential, was Maharishi Mahesh Yogi, of Transcendental Meditation fame, whose early disciples included some cultural heroes of major stature, including the Beatles. Yogi Bhajan, the Sikh master of Kundalini Yoga, arrived in 1968 and quickly attracted a Western following marked by their white turbans and energetic industry. Swami Muktananda, the charismatic guru who transmitted his powers by the touch of a peacock feather, came in 1970. *Shaktipat* denotes the transfer of psychospiritual power from guru to initiate through a touch or a glance. Guru Maharaj Ji, the adolescent "Lord of the Universe," arrived in 1971, announced the inauguration of the millennium in 1973, and quickly fell into oblivion.

The Tibetan Buddhist influx to the West, which followed the Communist annexation of Tibet, was also significant in the counterculture drift Eastward. Tarthang Talku Rinpoche arrived in 1969 and established the Tibetan Nyingma Meditation Center in Berkeley, California. Chogyam Trungpa Rinpoche set down on American soil in 1970 and founded the Karma Dzong Meditation Center and Naropa Institute at Boulder, Colorado.

The institute was a major forum for the syncretistic integration of his brand of Buddhism with the West. It regularly offered sessions featuring an impressive slate of guest faculty, from Allen Ginsberg to Norman Mailer.

Native-American religion and neopaganism. In 1968 Carlos Castaneda published *The Teachings of Don Juan: A Yaqui Way of Knowledge*. Thanks largely to his captivating stories, native-American shamanism joined the widening current of mystical/magical religiosity and fanned interest in native-American rituals and rites. Castaneda's tales offered an alternative within the alternative-reality traditions. The fantastical world of power animals, places of power, and spirit guides that Castaneda described was, no doubt, very appealing to those who were already weary and a little bored with contemplating the mystical void. Castaneda's universe was more interesting, simply because it was inhabited. But the principles that informed it were in essence the same as those of the Eastern schools.

Castaneda's South American sorcery was only one of the traditions oriented to the earth. Neopaganism, which held a natural attraction to a generation longing to return to the purity and simplicity of mother nature, also began to emerge in the 1970s. By the decade's end, it had blossomed into full-blown revival—the religion of choice for the ecologically minded and many spiritually inclined radical feminists.

Humanistic and transpersonal psychology. The forms that the new religious spirit took, however, were not always so clearly religious. Abraham Maslow, Fritz Perls, Carl Rogers, and Rollo May were key figures in the fledgling field of humanistic psychology. These men represented a new breed of psychologist that sought an alternative to the psychological orthodoxies of the day. Freudian psychoanalysis seemed to make humanity a victim of instinct and social conditioning; Skinnerian behavioralism made it a pawn in an environment of biological stimulus/response. The pioneers of humanistic psychology wanted to restore human dignity. What they offered was a psychology that glorified the self. It pronounced people's impulses essentially good, affirmed the unfathomable depths of human potential, and held out personal growth as an individual's highest goal. The affinities between the new psychology and mysticism did not go unnoticed, even by its founding fathers. Moving from vast to infinite potential and from personal growth to spiritual transformation required a virtually imperceptible shift.

Maslow, for one, placed the transcendent at the top of his list of hierarchical needs. He affirmed that humanity had a transcendent dimension that needed to be satisfied before self-actualization was complete. But the human longing for the transcendent was not, for Maslow, to be met by the wholly other God of biblical revelation. In fact, the transcendent dimension of which he spoke was not in the strictest sense an "other" at all: It was that dimension of an individual that intersected with the larger and more numinous realities of the cosmos. Maslow's self-actualized man was truly a self-satisfied man, a man fulfilled, who was full of himself.

Maslow's notion that human consciousness linked humanity with the fundamental realities of the universe became the basic premise of transpersonal psychology, the newest school in the psychological lineup.

If there is any ambiguity about humanistic psychology's alignment with the ancient wisdom, there is none about its transpersonal cousin, which has attracted intellectuals who can now spin out erudite analyses of humanity's higher dimensions under the aegis of institutions of higher learning.

There can be no question that humanistic psychology has changed the mental map of Western culture. Its influence has been far-reaching, its impact enormous. "So widespread have the assumptions of humanistic psychology become that people, by and large, can no longer frame an answer to the question of life's purpose except in terms of their own self-development" (Kilpatrick 1985, 148–149).

The elevation of personal growth as the highest good has had some predictably negative consequences. Humanistic psychology set out to construct a psychology of personal liberation;

what it delivered was a psychology of personal license and a rationale for asocial self-absorption:

> The trend in therapy toward a deification of the isolated self [shows] the ways in which selfishness and moral blindness now assert themselves . . . as enlightenment and psychic health. . . . It is in many ways the logical extension of the whole human potential movement . . . The refusal to consider moral complexities, the denial of history and a larger community, the disappearance of the Other, the exaggerations of the will. The reduction of all experience to a set of platitudes (Marin 1975, 45 ff.).

That, in brief, was the background and environment in which the New Age movement took shape. It was fed by many tributaries, but cannot be reduced to any single one. The New Age movement owes much to the traditions that preceded it, but has combined and expressed the teachings and practices of those traditions in novel and innumerable ways.

The strands of the ancient wisdom that came before the emergence of the NAM are now all aswirl, one virtually indistinguishable from the next, and all drawing on one another. The picture that surfaces is complex and, no doubt, confusing. But there are some discernible patterns that emerge upon closer inspection.

The New Age movement has exerted the most influence in areas where we are most vulnerable. It is no coincidence that it has made its greatest gains through the helping professions—psychology, in all its applications, and health care. Directing its efforts through those avenues accounts, in large measure, for the speed of its assimilation and the breadth of its influence. For the best way of changing the way people think, and thus behave, is not through coercion and abuse but "in the context of professionalism under the pretense of care" (Zimbardo 1984). That is true whether the motives are sinister or sincere, whether the ideology is sound or insane.

The New Age movement has successfully exploited that dynamic to fullest advantage, and in its success may lie an indirect indictment of the Church. For the New Age movement has advanced in those areas of concern that have traditionally been the Church's strength—compassionate care for those hurting in body and soul. Do the New Age gains in these areas reveal the Church's retreat? That, for the moment, must remain an open question.

What is not an open question is the scope of New Age spirituality and its pervasive presence in Western culture. The New Age movement is with us to stay. It is the wave of the future, because it has always been the way of the world.

2

A VISION FOR
A NEW HUMANITY

Robert J. L. Burrows

At the heart of the New Age vision is the conviction that humanity is poised between two ages. The perils of our time are interpreted not as the prelude to apocalyptic disaster, but to evolutionary transformation of the profoundest kind. Humanity, we are told, is at the crossroads, about to make a quantum leap forward and emerge as an entirely new creature, no longer constrained by the limitations and evils of the old order.

Understandably, mapping out the differences between the two ages and explaining the dynamic of change between them is a major preoccupation of New Age authors. Fritjof Capra's *The Turning Point* (1982) is representative of numerous books that attempt to do just that. Capra is one of the more popular New Age writers, whose books have gained wide exposure.

In *The Turning Point*, Capra provides a critique of Western culture that is sometimes sound. He also describes changes in various fields of knowledge, often with a measure of validity. But the book at base is an argument for the ancient wisdom's assessment of the human predicament: All human ills stem from an inability to perceive reality's unity. That is the key to understanding the human dilemma and the dynamic behind the process of human history. For Capra and his confreres, history is not the story of humanity's Fall into sin and its restoration by God's saving acts; history is the story of humanity's fall into ignorance and gradual ascent into enlightenment. It is a chronicle of humanity's changing perceptions, from a mind that divides to a mind undivided—the emergence of the latter marking history's culmination, the dawning of a New Age.

Capra charts Western culture's changing paradigms—the models it uses to perceive reality—precisely along these lines. He links the old order and the crises of our time to a paradigm informed by Newtonian physics, rationalism, and the Judeo-Christian tradition. Each, he argues, has contributed to our present crises because each has failed to see reality as a interrelated whole.

Newtonian physics gave us a mechanistic view of a world whose fundamental building blocks were billiard-ball-like atoms, separate and distinct. Rationalism exalted reason, which by its nature, Capra argues, is linear, unable to grasp reality's unity. And the Judeo-Christian tradition severs God from creation, desacralizing it and opening it to exploitation.

But seeing the world in a fragmented fashion is not Capra's only complaint. He sees the tendency of Newtonian physics and reason to divide reality into unrelated bits as a masculine trait that finds extreme expression in the patriarchical character of the Judeo-Christian religion. While its authoritative male God prevailed, authoritarianism—centralized power and hierarchical social organization—was the order of the day.

What does Capra hold out as the remedy? A culture based on a paradigm that recognizes reality's unity and sees things holistically. Such a paradigm, Capra maintains, is taking shape. It has its roots in nuclear physics, which views fundamental reality as a seamless web of vibrant, pulsating energy; intuitive means of knowing, which grasp the whole directly, without the mediation of reason; and a feminine spirituality "based on awareness of the oneness of all living forms and of their cyclical rhythms of birth and death" (Capra 1982, 415). This paradigm, Capra argues, will restore creation and heal humanity's alienation. With a nurturing goddess as the cultural image of deity, decentralized power and egalitarian social organization will unfold.

The goddess motif is not as prominent in other New Age writings, but the basic ingredients of this revisionist history are invariably present. And it is revisionist history, because it distorts the past and sometimes ignores it altogether. It's revisionist history because it's pressed into a preconceived pattern to buttress a foregone conclusion.

Capra's argument is clever and compelling, but its premise—that the mystic's holistic vision of reality will save us—flies in the face of an incontrovertible fact: Where it has flourished, the mystical vision has patently *not* produced social utopia. India is a case in point. The vision Capra believes will deliver us seems to thrive in cultures that are in a perpetual state of disarray, where misery is rampant and corruption rife. The problem is human perversity, not human perception. The pivotal issue is holiness, not holism; the only antidote is God's redemptive and re-creative grace in Christ.

Restructuring the Mind

Historical analysis is certainly not the only area where the New Age assessment of the human predicament crops up. It runs through all the NAM does and says. That assessment is the basis for a host of programs aimed at our psychological ills. Werner Erhard's *est*, established in 1971, was one of the first and most successful self-motivational packages to appear. Over 500,000 people have had the *est* experience, including such celebrities as Yoko Ono and John Denver.

Erhard had a checkered background that involved some serious dabbling in Scientology, Mind Dynamics, and Zen. When he got "it," he guessed others would want it and decided gentle persuasion was not the most effective means of giving it away. What he forcefully delivered was a radical version of the mystical vision: Whatever givens reality seems to have are imposed by belief. Reality is make-believe, because belief is what makes it. Whatever an individual experiences is, therefore, that individual's own creation. As psychologist, business consultant, and *est* enthusiast Adelaide Bry says (1975, 146), "Every human being bears the responsibility for 'sourcing' his own life. In this way, as source, each one of us is ' God.' " That is radical responsibility—and a radical denial of the real world.

There is no question that we interpret our experiences, and in that sense, the interpretations are ours. But interpreting reality and *creating* reality are two entirely different matters. There is even a measure of humility in the former that is not in the latter. After all, if we interpret reality, our interpretation could be wrong, but if wrong, we have the option of going back and testing it against a reality that is really there. However if the reality we experience is self-created, there is no room for self-doubt, absolutely no margin for error, nor any possibility of mercy. Whether it is rape or rapture, there is no one to credit or blame but ourselves. A heartless, inhuman determinism is where Erhard's self-created universe heads and many times is where it ends up. It is a quick, cruel answer to the mystery of evil in the world, all the pain and suffering life entails.

Erhard's carefully crafted seminar is one of a multitude of means to clear the mind of its crippling clutter and shift consciousness into transformative gear. Drugs, music, chanting, ritual, and guided imagery may all be used to the same end. The possibilities are literally infinite and may even appear contradictory.

Sensory deprivation. At one end of the extreme spectrum is sensory deprivation. And among the more popular methods for tuning out the world is the flotation tank. In the darkness and silence of the flotation tank, practically all external stimuli are eliminated, even one's sense of gravity. That kind of environment is bound to bring about extraordinary experiences. It may even do some people some good, especially those who never seem able to stop and take a breath. But the flotation-tank experience can be interpreted in the context of the New Age worldview, and often is. In the foreword to John Lilly's *The Deep Self* (1977, 17–18), Craig S. Enright, a medical doctor, does just that:

> Entering an isolation tank is much easier than getting into most spaceships. . . . Inside the tank . . . you are suspended in embryonic silence one hundred million miles out in deep space, and suddenly the Logos, the Universal Vibration, begins to pervade the fabric of awareness, coming at once from inside and from all directions.

Self-mortification. Sensory deprivation is at one end of the scale; the self-mortification rituals of Fakir Musafar are definitely at the other end. Musafar, also know as Roland Loomis, is an ad executive and self-proclaimed "modern primitive" who pursues spiritual fulfillment through the reenactment of ancient rituals. He appears in Dan and Mark Jury's film *Dances Sacred and Profane*. In one of the sequences, Musafar reenacts the Sundance ceremony that actor Richard Harris depicted in the 1970 film *A Man Called Horse*. Musafar puts large, needlelike pins into his chest, ties them to ropes bound to branches of a cottonwood tree, leans back, and hangs suspended in the air for hours, until the skin breaks and he falls to the ground. For Musafar, the exercise is spiritual, its effect, pure bliss: "When we were out on the bluff . . . had you said 'Roland' or 'Fakir' to me, I wouldn't have answered. I was the wind. I was a rock. To go into these spaces you have to leave your ego and your identity behind. You're hyperconscious" (Guthmann 1986, 35).

Meditation. Musafar's technique for tuning into the spiritual dimensions of the cosmos is, to say the least, a little bizarre. The more commonly known methods, and more frequently used, are those inherited from Eastern mystical traditions: various forms of meditation, accompanied by physical, breathing, and relaxation exercises. In their original setting, the religious intent of these practices is transparent. They are used to bring about states of consciousness that are identified with ultimate reality in its pure, featureless, unmanifest form. In such states, individual consciousness *is* ultimate reality, embodying all the wisdom and power of deity.

That premise, however, is not always easy to detect, because it is not always explicitly stated. That omission is sometimes intentional, as it was with Maharishi Mahesh Yogi and Transcendental Meditation. Maharishi passed his TM off as scientific, emphasizing its ability to reduce stress. What he did not tell his prospective customers was that petting your dog has a similar effect. He also did not tell them it was religion they were getting.

The Yogi had a good marketing sense and knew what would sell. He could not, however, relinquish his traditional Hindu roots, and the TM initiation ceremony, with its invocation of Hindu deities, gave his religious intent away. But New Age adherents generally have no such attachments to Maharishi's, or any other, religious tradition. Consequently, the premises of the ancient wisdom have been extracted from their original spiritual context, and the religious trappings and terminology have all but disappeared.

An example from the business arena is a good case in point. A Stanford business professor recently put his class through its paces. To improve entrepreneurial creativity and intuition, his students were coached through a guided meditation. They were told to let go of all judgments, obstructing thoughts, past perceptions, "whatever is keeping you from tapping that reservoir of magnificence within you" (Tanner 1983, 18). On the recommended reading list were books about Zen, Yoga, the Tao Te Ching, and one title, *I Am That,* by Swami Muktananda.

If the recommended reading list had not been mentioned, the worldview assumptions informing the exercise might have gone unnoticed by an observer or even by the participants, but the assumptions are there; intuition is operative when the mind is swept clean. That much is stated, and even that is debatable.

What is not stated, but implied, is that information available in such states, like ultimate truth itself, is not available to ordinary consciousness. The mystical worldview supplies the reason: Only when the mind is stilled of all that fragments and divides can reality be apprehended without confusing interference. Only when individual consciousness dissolves into the consciousness of the cosmos is it possible to intuitively respond to the demands of the moment with undistracted precision. The individual is no longer in the way, and the universe can express itself directly, without the mind's distorting influences.

Richard Moss puts the principle succinctly: "When I am there God is gone; when I am gone God is there" (1983). That principle guides New Age understanding, whether the end in view is intuition, creativity, contacting the inner self or spirit guides, or simply reaching for enlightenment.

Without the use of any explicit spiritual terminology, the students at Stanford were introduced to an interpretation of intuition that dovetailed perfectly with the New Age worldview. That in itself may not be remarkable. But the class on intuition is only one among innumerable exposures that will subtly, and sometimes not so subtly, condition those students to think in categories consistent with that worldview. What is true of them is true of the culture as a whole, for New Age conceptions about mental states and the mind's power can be found in every field, from health to sports, from business to education.

Tuning the Body

The premises of the ancient wisdom are also at the root of the New Age attitude toward the body. Like the mind, the body is considered a receptor and transmitter of cosmic forces, and a repository of the good and ill effects of life's experiences. It is also considered a key instrument in the quest for self-deification, and must be carefully tuned.

Tuning the body to the forces of the cosmos is Yoga's intent in its traditional context. It is also the purpose of many diet, exercise, massage, and movement therapies that come under the holistic-health umbrella. The merits of these alternatives to Western medicine vary, but all are invariably informed by a particular perspective on how the body, mind, spirit, and cosmos are related. That perspective has little to do with science, though it is often passed off as such. It has everything to do with the basic premises of the New Age worldview.

A myriad of diagnostic and curative techniques are founded on the New Age premise that reality is one and manifests itself as spiritual energy in the body—as in all creation. While it is true that all bodily parts are interrelated, the human organism cannot be reduced to such simplistic formulas.

Reflexology is one technique based on that erroneous notion. It rests on the premise that the foot serves as the window onto internal bodily parts. Massage a point on the foot, reflexology maintains, and a diseased organ, seemingly far removed, will reap the benefit. Reflexology is one of the more popular massage techniques, no doubt because foot massage is an enjoyable experience. It is sure to do the feet some good, in spite of the bogus nature of its other claims.

Reflexology is only one item in the holistic-health lineup: Iridology, acupuncture, acupressure, Reiki, and Therapeutic Touch are a few more. These alternative therapies may have some success, but not for the reasons given. Those who benefit from a therapy, however, are likely to see any improvement as confirmation of the worldview used to explain it. Benefits, however, are not always forthcoming. When the claims are extravagant and the illness serious, relying solely on alternative medicine could literally be deadly.

Practical Magic

The same premises of the ancient wisdom undergird more traditional occult practices revived in New Age circles. With these, the human instrument is not directly manipulated. Objects are employed whose patterns of energy and vibration supposedly resonate with those of mind and body, bringing about benefits ranging from curing insomnia and breast cancer to aiding business transactions or smoothing stormy relationships.

Rock crystals are high on the list of desirable commodities. The demand for them has, in fact, created a substantial and lucrative market. For one company, Star Magic, sales have tripled over the past four years (Smilgis 1987, 66). How is the alleged power of the rock understood? One crystal promoter explains: "Quartz originates as a thought form in the universal mind on the higher levels of light and is projected down to the earthly substance that quartz is and will become. Crystals serve as a connector to those higher realms of light, and are an access tool to other planes of awareness—a 'window of light' to higher realms" (Sutphen 1987, 14).

Crystals are only one of the literally endless possibilities. Pyramids, colors, and flower essences are often understood in a similar way and used for similar ends.

Spiritism

The body, mind, and more traditional occult practices can all serve as the "medium" for New Age transformation. Mediumship in the more familiar sense is also a New Age vogue, picking up momentum as the years go by. Contacting spirits of the dead is not a significant concern. But spiritism in one form or another is a typical New Age mainstay, if only because of its universality among the traditions from which the New Age draws its inspiration. In Western occult and Eastern mystical traditions, the cosmos is frequently seen as a multidimensional reality inhabited by spirits of various descriptions. Those spirits are considered a source of power, instruction, and guidance for anyone who knows the techniques of enlisting their services.

Mediumship in the more traditional vein is not uncommon. In fact, some of the New Age movement's notables have fallen under the sway of mediums professing to be channels of enlightened entities. Ram Dass was wooed by Joya Santanya, who served as a conduit for his former guru. In the late seventies, Esalen, the New Age experimental center for intellectuals on the leading edge, submitted itself to the higher wisdom of the "Nine," who dispensed truth and advice through medium-in-residence Jenny O'Connor (Klein 1979, 26–33). Even hospice pioneer Elisabeth Kübler-Ross could not resist the lure of spiritism. She became a supporter of Jay Barham, a self-appointed medium of questionable repute, and found comforting confidantes in a number of spirit guides (Fuentes 1979).

It is a striking irony that those who so loudly bruited the message of the divine within ended up seeking counsel from spirits on the outside. The conclusion is inescapable: They went inside and, like the rest of us, found themselves wanting. Divinity is a burden that humanity simply cannot bear.

Ram Dass and Esalen have since severed ties with these other-worldly messengers. It seems they were not taken to new spiritual heights, but were simply taken in. Such naïveté among people of otherwise great intelligence is understandable when the only criteria for discernment is a fuzzy subjectivity.

But even subjective impressions, which may sometimes be right on another principle, are not to be trusted. For in occult and mystical traditions, a spiritual teacher will sometimes throw contradictions, bizarre and even immoral behavior in the pilgrim's path, to shake the pilgrim free of all preconceptions of reality. Needless to say, it is a principle that removes any possible ground for criticism and makes those who adopt it dangerously vulnerable to exploitation.

The connection with the spirit world has also yielded a number of writings with influence extending beyond New Age circles. In a popular vein, there is Richard Bach's spirit-inspired *Jonathan Livingston Seagull* and Jane Robert's *Seth Speaks* series—older works, but still with us. The three-volume *Course in Miracles* "dictated" to Helen Schucman is more significant because it is more insidious. This hefty work, allegedly communicated by Jesus Christ, is couched in biblical terminology and sounds deceptively Christian. But it is a rehash of the metaphysics common to nineteenth-century New Thought. It presents a Gnostic view of this world, where forgiveness comes easily with the knowledge that there is never anything to forgive; where guilt is quickly dismissed with the recognition that the real self is unsulliable, impossible to taint. *A Course in Miracles* has met with bubbling enthusiasm and gained widespread exposure through the popular writings of Gerald Jampolsky, and it is, unfortunately, gaining a toehold in the Church.

New Age Spiritism, like the Spiritualism of the nineteenth-century, is fueled in no small degree by the desire for hard evidence of humanity's immortality. Data on near-death experiences (like that published by Raymond Moody in *Life After Life*) and widespread belief in reincarnation are also consistent with that tradition. They all remove death's sting, not by pointing to Christ's substitutionary death and resurrection, but by denying death's reality and ruling out the possibility of divine judgment from the outset. As one New Age author says: "Death is the Great teacher . . . teaching us that there can be no death" (Aronson 1983, 8–10). What used to summon our guilt before God and remind us of our mortal frame, as one commentator puts it, now begins to "sound better than a trip to Disneyland" (Coleman 1979, 43).

Shirley MacLaine is to be counted among those in hot pursuit of entities from the far side. She is an avid devotee of Ramtha, purportedly a 35,000-year-old ascended master, who uses J. Z. Knight to convey his messages. Ramtha has just issued a book—proof that even if you perish, you can still publish—containing some very old insights. Here's a sampling of the wisdom of Ramtha's years: "God . . . has never been *outside* of you—it *is* you." "God, of itself, is wholly without goodness or evil . . . God simply is." "I am here to help you realize that you are an ongoing immortal essence." "There is no voice that will *ever* teach you greater than your own. . . . Who you are this day is the answer to *everything* you have ever wanted" (Weinberg 1986). Old wisdom, indeed, reiterating the lie of the tempter at history's dawn: "You shall not die . . . you shall be as gods" (*see*

Genesis 3:4, 5). Whatever other information may be dispensed, the affirmation of humanity's deity and the denial of death are the messages universally delivered by envoys from the spirit world.

J. Z. Knight, the channel of Shirley MacLaine's choice, has received a considerable boost in reputation and, no doubt, a strategic marketing advantage since MacLaine's *Out on a Limb* and *Dancing in the Light* have materialized. The TV version of Shirley's *Out on a Limb* occult odyssey has further fanned the flames of this latest cultural fad. The channelers and the entities who speak through them, to borrow an apt biblical phrase, are legion. Ramtha, Emmanuel, Lazarus, Michael, Jonah are just a few of the entities who are now getting through, pulling large audiences with money to pay. All this would be laughable, if it were not taken seriously. But the audiences the channelers command and the sale of books related to the subject indicate a sober curiosity that is itself sobering.

The assimilation of New Age assumptions and beliefs is going on at all levels of contemporary culture, and mass entertainment is both a fair measure and effective means of that assimilation. The *Star Wars* saga of creative genius George Lucas comes to mind in that connection. Luke Skywalker's initiation into the league of Jedi knights involves mastering the "force" that animates the cosmos, dwells within, and is tapped intuitively through feelings. That itself is a good grade-school primer of the ancient wisdom. Sights and sounds of the *Star Wars* trilogy are rattling around in the brains of millions of Americans. It was a forceful series that communicated the message of the "force" to more than a few.

What Lies Ahead

The New Age movement is real and pervasive; it is not about to go away. As its beliefs and practices continue to be assimilated into the general culture, mingle with compatible currents, and tug at the natural inclinations of the fallen human heart, it can do nothing but grow. And that growth, in the end, must have largely negative consequences, for the religion that deifies the natural order, as the New Age movement does, deifies whatever comes naturally—both humanity's loftiest ideals and its basest impulses. Any limitations imposed, as those in the New Age never tire of saying, are by definition arbitrary. Any act, no matter how laudable or perverse, is potentially a sacrament, a gate that opens onto the numinous. New Age advocates are not generally consistent with that premise. In many instances, they are meeting legitimate needs of people and addressing issues sometimes passed over by Christendom—like the good Samaritan, whose theology was askew but whose actions were right.

But something of what may be ahead is already here. The *Utne Reader* recently ran an article entitled "Re-Vamping the World: On the Return of the Holy Prostitute." The article by Deena Metzger was delivered at a Conference of Feminist Art and Culture in the eighties held at California State University in Long Beach. It is a serious and reasoned argument for exactly what the title suggests: A reinstatement of the holy prostitute as the conduit of the sacred. Metzger, however, does not have simply temple attendants in mind. She is advocating the role for *all* women as a means of resacralizing the body and regaining feminine spiritual power lost with the advent of patriarchical religion. "The task is to accept . . . sexuality and erotic love as spiritual disciplines, to believe that eros is pragmatic" (Metzger 1985, 123).

Entertaining that idea is shocking enough, even if perfectly consistent with Metzger's premises. But the responses the article received were even more disturbing. Some objected strenuously; others, however, applauded unabashedly. It is this kind of blatant decadence against which the NAM can provide no defense. Dostoyevski said that anything is permissible if there is no God. Anything is also permissible if *everything* is God. The article is a sign of the times and a sign of things to come.

Metzger's radical measures represent the extreme fringe of the NAM. Her particular scenario is not about to be embraced by a large portion of the general public or the Christian community—at least not at the moment. It is the broader, wider stream of the NAM, which is less easily seen, that is influencing our culture to think in typically New Age ways: Ways that glorify the self, deny the reality of human depravity, and hold out pure, contentless experience as ultimate truth.

The foundation for the broader, wider stream is not particularly new. Ironically, New Age spirituality echoes, and is a logical extension of, the secularism it repudiates. Both deny the reality of the Creator, and both see humanity as the final arbiter of truth and value. New Age spirituality simply heightens secularism's mistakes by inflating humanity's significance, yielding what Brooks Alexander dubs "cosmic humanism."

There is another irony in all this. It concerns the cultural conditions in which the New Age movement arose and in which its predecessors flourished. As the occult historian James Webb notes, the occult enthusiasm of the nineteenth and early twentieth centuries erupted during times of acute social crisis. Rapid social and economic change and two world wars combined to instill widespread fear. The alternative-reality traditions represented an attempt to bring meaning and stability back into a shattered and disoriented world.

What was true of the New Age movement's predecessors is no less true of the New Age movement today. The cultural crisis in the West has continued unabated: the disintegration of the family; the loss of a sense of place in a society always on the move; the absence of myths and rituals marking the passages of life from cradle to grave; the erosion of moral values that govern and build relationships. These are a few of the factors that have thrown the Western psyche into confusion and fear, heightened by the ever-present threat of nuclear holocaust and the pillage and plunder of the planet.

But the dissolution of boundaries, limitations, and taboos, which signals a culture in crisis, is precisely what New Age spirituality encourages and holds out as humanity's hope: The dissolution of all distinctions in the ultimate "one." That is why Christopher Lasch calls it the ideology of resignation, in spite of its air of optimism (1977, 9 ff.). It is an ideology that reinforces cultural confusion by exalting it as ultimate truth. Thus, the pervasiveness of New Age ideology is a yardstick for cultural decay; its advance, a measure of Western culture's decline.

In the context of Western history, the emergence of the New Age movement is no surprise. The rise of rationalism and the secularism it gave birth to emptied Western culture of all its gods, Christian and pagan alike. But humanity without religion is like a camel without its hump. It was only a matter of time until the spirits once again returned. A spirituality that simultaneously extended the secular ideology already in place, reinforced the chaos of sociological realities, and pandered to human hubris was the most likely candidate for mass appeal. For all those reasons and then some, when the West found religion again, it was not, by and large, the religion of biblical Christianity, but that of the New Age.

In the sweep of Western history, what we see unfolding is the scenario Paul describes in Romans 1: the rejection of God, the Creator and Redeemer; the subsequent deification of creation; and the ensuing degradation of humanity and cultural decay. With the emergence of the New Age movement, what G. K. Chesterton once said, describing the same dynamic, is again proven true: "When a man ceases to believe in God, he does not believe in nothing, he believes in anything." In contemporary history, the "anything" he believes in is represented by all that comes under the rubric "New Age," however sophisticated or crude.

Guidelines for Discernment

Because of the scope of its concerns, the range of its applications, and the variety of its expressions, the New Age movement is often difficult to detect. Even if detected, it is difficult to assess. How do you spot genuine New Age influence? Once you've spotted it, what do you do?

These are hard, complex questions that do not yield quick

and easy answers. There are, however, some broad guidelines.

The New Age movement has a typical vocabulary, typical political concerns, and engages in a host of typical practices. With some exceptions, none of these in themselves provide adequate criteria for identifying New Age influence. The difficulty arises because the same vocabulary, political concerns, and practices can be informed by various worldviews.

It is true that certain words occur with predictable regularity in New Age writings: *holistic, holographic, synergistic, unity, oneness, transformation, personal growth, human potential, awakening, networking, energy, consciousness.* But it would be erroneous to conclude that these words always indicate New Age commitment. What significance words have largely depends on those who use them. Single buzzwords or phrases are inadequate for determining worldview orientation; a wider interpretive context is required.

A similar argument applies to New Age political concerns. New Age advocates are typically for ecology, against nuclear weapons, and for grass-roots democracy. Being typically New Age, however, does not imply all those who take similar positions are aligned with the New Age movement. Those positions can be arrived at through ideologies that are diametrically opposed. Marx and Jesus were both concerned with the poor. That does not make Marx a Christian or Jesus a Communist. A concern for ecology, similarly, does not of itself indicate either a commitment to a deified creation or the Deity of creation. Nor are issues rendered illegitimate simply because New Age enthusiasts typically address them. There is good biblical warrant for being ecologically minded, as there is for many other concerns that draw New Age attention. There is also good biblical warrant for rejecting outright the monistic premises that inform the New Age agenda.

New Age political concerns and common New Age terminology raise questions of discernment. But New Age therapies, programs, and practices are more vexatious, if only because they are so numerous. When overtly religious, they may seem compatible with Christian faith. When inconspicuously secular, they may seem spiritually neutral. In attempting to come to some conclusion about a program or therapy, Christians need to assess two elements: practice and interpretation.

Some New Age practices are outrightly condemned by Scripture and should be avoided. For example, spiritism and various forms of divination (see Deuteronomy 18: 9–12). From a biblical perspective, everything that seems supernatural does not necessarily find its source in God.

Some practices, such as those that use abusive and manipulative psychological techniques, are morally objectionable and are to be rejected on that account alone.

Other practices may seem neutral and, because of beneficial effects, even desirable, but the interpretive framework in which those practices are imbedded makes them problematic. The body therapies are a good illustration of that ambiguity. Massage in itself is not a bad thing and can have some marvelous effects. But when the masseur gives a play-by-play and talks about manipulating deep tissue to realign the energy of your aura, you know you're getting more than a rubdown. Should you jump off the table and run out the door? There's no easy answer to that question, either.

The situation with the masseur is analogous to the New Testament problem of eating meat that had been sacrificed to idols and then sold in the market. Should you, or shouldn't you? The early Church said it was a matter of individual conscience. In the New Age context, that must be our answer, too. But if alternatives exist that are not so spiritually loaded, those are the ones to pursue first.

Everyday we make transactions and solicit services from people who hold unbiblical beliefs. The same questions apply whether you are dealing with the New Age masseur or the secular humanist who owns the Safeway store. But in the case of the Safeway owner, there is less chance that you'll think the wonderful experience you've had filling your shopping cart validates his interpretation of the world. You would be more inclined to do that if the benefits were of a more direct and personal nature, like massage or a cancer cure. The areas that hold out the greatest potential for benefit are the areas of our greatest vulnerability. Benefits in those areas will be more readily taken as confirmation of the worldview used to explain them. It is in those areas that caution and vigilance are most required.

Because of the variety and scope of New Age programs, it is impossible to list criteria that would serve as a basis for recognizing the unbiblical worldview that undergirds them all. Worldview is, however, the key ingredient. Knowing your own is essential for detecting another's. Exercising discernment is to become a worldview watcher. That means asking questions about meaning: What is explicitly stated or implied about the nature of God, the nature of humanity, and the relationship between them? That is the surest ground for assessment. More specific advice is difficult to give. As a general rule of thumb, be particularly worldview attentive if a therapy, seminar, or workshop: 1. is explained in terms of harmonizing, manipulating, integrating, or balancing energies or polarities; 2. denigrates the value of the mind or belief or; 3. makes extravagant claims. If it seems too good to be true, it probably is.

There is another area of consideration that needs further comment. It revolves around the question: What practices typically employed by New Agers can be engaged in by Christians?

It is clear that not everything those of the New Age use to tune into cosmic forces comes with monistic premises attached. The mystical mind set, in fact, can be brought to bear on any human activity. The spate of books on Zen gives some indication of what can be assimilated and pressed into the service of divine illumination. There is Zen and the Art of Motorcycle Maintenance, The Zen of Running, and The Zen of Flower Arrangement. Obviously, those activities can be engaged in without reference to Zen Buddhism. It is certainly not unbiblical to maintain a motorcycle, run, or arrange flowers; Christians can do so to their hearts' content. Problems arise, however, when jogging moves from the street into the sanctuary, to be used as a vehicle for worship.

Such is the case with "guided imagery" and relaxation exercises that are increasingly being used in Christian circles. They are two practices, among many, that raise similar questions. A good case could be made for tracing the popularity of these methods to the influence of the New Age movement or its spiritual cousins, who use them constantly for spiritual ends. However, more often than not, the influence is indirect, and those who employ these methods do not necessarily hold New Age beliefs.

Guided imagery and relaxation exercises no doubt have a legitimate sphere of function. Unimaginative, tense believers are not the biblical goal. But when used for devotional purposes, these practices raise theological questions that need to be addressed. Is it possible to use guided imagery and relaxation exercises as aids to worship? Is it possible to use them to communicate with God or receive revelations from Him? Or do those who use these techniques inevitably fall into magical manipulation and spiritual idolatry?

Whatever the answers, the presence of guided imagery and other new arrivals in the Christian community is somewhat unsettling. They seem to point to a Church that has lost touch with its rich spiritual heritage, and, in its hunger for a deeper spiritual life, absorbs whatever is in the cultural wind, with blusterous indiscrimination. The times demand more than that. Christ requires more. The vitality of the Church and the hope of the world may very well depend upon it.

PART TWO

THE FLOWERING
OF THE
NEW AGE—
ASSIMILATION

3

HOLISTIC HEALTH: MARCUS WELBY ENTERS THE NEW AGE

Paul C. Reisser, M.D.

"THE IMPENDING TRANSFORMATION OF MEDICINE IS A WINDOW TO THE transformation of all our institutions" (Ferguson 1980, 241). This pronouncement aptly expressed the early euphoria of New Agers who saw holistic health as a vigorous young David rising to challenge the Goliath of Western medicine. Indeed, Ferguson's optimism did not seem unfounded.

Before 1975, hardly anyone had heard the term *holistic*. But by 1980, when Ferguson's manifesto was published, thousands were traveling to conferences in all parts of the country to hear renowned speakers like Jonas Salk and Norman Cousins describe a radically new vision for health. Holistic health centers were sprouting up all over the United States. Alternative therapies such as meditation, biofeedback, and laying on of hands were gaining some respectability in medical literature. More importantly, New Agers were receiving favorable coverage in newspapers and popular magazines.

Goliath, however, has remained very much alive, challenged far more by the cost of his insurance armor than by any New Age shepherd. Meanwhile, David is looking for new recruits and more effective stones to fling. So far, few of his missiles have made much of a dent in the health-care system. They have, however, made an impact on popular culture. Ultimately, for the New Age movement, that is where the money is.

Without question, health and illness are key issues of the New Age movement. A serious illness triggers intense soul-searching, a review of values, and even questions about the meaning of life and death that New Agers are more than happy to answer. But illnesses that aren't so serious provide a much broader patch of fertile ground for holistic health.

Every day, millions of people suffer from symptoms such as fatigue, headaches, palpitations, and abdominal pains. When they consult their doctors, they are usually told there is nothing wrong—that is, a general exam, lab tests, and X-ray studies reveal no obvious disease. The problem, in fact, may be tied to life-style. The patient may be eating too much (or eating the wrong things), exercising too little, coping poorly with stress, or simply be bored with life.

Others are actually sick or dying, as a result of their own everyday choices. Indeed, most of the plagues of the twentieth century—cardiovascular disease, stroke, diabetes, cancer, arthritic disorders, and more recently AIDS—have links to behavior. But there is no vaccine for bad habits or no new technology that can undo the results of thousands of personal decisions.

The frustration generated by modern medicine's trench warfare against degenerative and life-style-created disease is magnified by soaring health-care costs, which now total about ten percent of the United States gross national product. Coincidentally, many Americans are quietly rethinking their relationships with institutions and authority figures that were highly esteemed in the past.

In his 1982 best-seller, *Megatrends* (131, 133), John Naisbitt wrote:

> For decades, institutions such as the government, the medical establishment, the corporation and the school system were America's buffer against life's hard realities—the needs for food, housing, health care, education—as well as its mysteries—birth, illness, death. . . Slowly we began to wean ourselves off our collective institutional dependence, learning to trust and rely only on ourselves.

All of this has provided a field day for the promoters of the New Age, who have worked with fervor to bring their solution—holistic health—before the people of the Western world. Yet, as with their other areas of activity, New Agers are far less interested in reforming the way health care is provided than they are in changing the worldview of its patients. The importance of this fact cannot be overstated.

Beneath the appealing concern for "healing the total person— body, mind and spirit" lies a compulsion to bring radical change to the way we view all of life. This compulsion also fuels most of the alternative therapies that flourish in the holistic movement. Unfortunately, many who are attracted to the unfurled banners proclaiming wholeness and wellness, or who may simply be fed up with expensive, impersonal medical care, are unaware of the total package they may unwrap when they toy with New Age medicine.

Admittedly, recognizing that a particular technique, practitioner, or organization belongs to the New Age movement may be difficult. We must look beyond titles, and even beyond spelling. Someone who claims to be "holistic" may or may not be a New Ager, but changing the spelling to "wholistic" does not guarantee a neutral worldview.

In order to be discerning, we need to scratch beneath the

surface of a therapy or organization to see its roots and, more importantly, its intentions. This is easier said than done, but we can take a step in the right direction by understanding how four basic presuppositions of the New Age movement are expressed in holistic health.

All Is One

At the heart of the New Age movement is monism, the belief that everything in the universe is a vast, undifferentiated, impersonal unity. This unity may be called "the one," or "Universal Consciousness," or "Life Energy," or in deference to less-enlightened souls, it may even be called "God." But whatever it is called, it is said to be the primal fabric of the universe—and of us.

In our materialistic, technology-saturated Western culture, such an idea may not seem intuitively obvious. Most of us do not readily appreciate being lumped together with a brick wall, a blue sky, or our pet cat. That is why, according to the New Agers, we can only "experience" (if not exactly understand) this ultimate unity via an altered state of consciousness. Normal waking awareness, the state we are presented with in this life, seems to be a definite barrier to New Age enlightenment.

Whether experienced or taken on faith, monism is the basis for a number of New Age therapies. At a holistic-health conference, you might hear the following line of reasoning, which leads toward monism:

> Western medicine has been built on a process of dividing the human being into systems, organs, organ components, cells, intracellular organs, and biochemical reactions. In order to understand how something works, a researcher will usually try to break it down and analyze the pieces. (Indeed, one of the first projects for new medical students is to dissect a human body.) This process has generated a

vast body of medical information and led to a pro-
liferation of specialists and subspecialists over the
past thirty years. Unfortunately, in the mountain of
data, modern medicine sometimes loses track of the
patient.

Holistic medicine starts from a different direction.
It assumes that we are more than a collection of
organ systems or biochemical reactions. We are
body, mind, and spirit, all interconnected into a
whole that is greater than the sum of its parts. Illness
and wellness can both be understood only when we
keep in perspective the totality of life. Sickness
represents more than a passive yielding to maraud-
ing bacteria, and recovery is more than a response to
miracle drugs. Ultimately, we alone are responsible
for our own illness or wellness.

So far, so good. Indeed, even the medical establishment,
sluggish as it is to change, has begun to think in similar
directions. Since 1970, family practice, the medical specialty
most overtly geared to the whole patient, has undergone a
virtual revival. Today, most hospitals provide a wide range of
wellness-oriented programs for their patients and the community at large. The importance to human health of eating habits,
exercise, response to stress, substance abuse, sexual behavior,
goals, friendships, and attitudes is now discussed more widely
than ever before.

Unfortunately, the New Age line of reasoning goes quite a bit
further than this. Since modern physics has shown that matter
and energy are different forms of the same stuff, New Age
reasoning concludes that everything, including human beings,
is in essence congealed energy. That energy is, in turn, connected to a universal "life energy" that flows throughout the
world and the universe under a variety of aliases: *prana*, Ch'i,
bioplasma, "the force." Thus, say the New Agers, if we really
want to promote health, we must learn how to manipulate this
invisible flow of energy.

Holistic therapies often center on such techniques. For instance, acupuncture and acupressure, using carefully placed needles or localized massage, are said to manipulate the flow of Ch'i through invisible channels in the body called meridians. Another holistic therapy is applied kinesiology, which is used by a limited but fervent number of chiropractors. The aim of this technique is to diagnose problems in energy flow by using tests of muscle strength. Then there is Therapeutic Touch, which is widely promoted among nurses. Therapeutic Touch claims to infuse *prana* (the Hindu version of universal energy) into patients. Yoga is another technique that allegedly manipulates the flow of *prana*.

Promoters of such holistic therapies rarely seem concerned about the lack of reliable data to support their claims. Some even state that their techniques are primarily intuitive and can't be understood by an analytical approach. Others, however, believe that scientific research will someday "catch up" with what they are doing.

Most of them merely point to their satisfied clients. If people are being helped, what does it matter if the scientific establishment agrees with a technique?

It matters a great deal.

If independent researchers can show the flow of Ch'i (or any other universal energy) to be a reality of human physiology, we should all seek to understand and manipulate it. In fact, we should rewrite our biology textbooks and channel research funds toward unraveling the link between primal energy and health. But this is not the case. Since the only supporting evidence for the New Age's "All Is One" theory consists of anecdotes, ancient manuscripts, and altered states of consciousness, we should think of these therapies as the mystical or religious experiences they are, not as medical treatments.

Humans Are Divine

New Age theory continues by saying that since "All Is One," we must be part of the one, and therefore we are all gods (or

God), even though our everyday experiences may not exactly bear that out.

Several New Age therapies spring from this reasoning. The idea is simple: If we can be convinced that we are ultimately perfect and "one with the universe," then physical (and other) healing will take place. Better results will come if we can actually experience oneness through an altered state of consciousness.

This is really not a new concept. For the past century, several "mind science" groups, such as Christian Science, Religious Science, Science of Mind, have been setting forth similar teachings. For instance, Mary Baker Eddy, in the Christian Science textbook *Science and Health*, taught that the material world was unreal, an "error" created and maintained by our collective "mortal mind." Her key to overcoming illness was denying the reality of matter (as well as sin, sickness, and death), and affirming that we are perfect spiritual beings. This strongly foreshadows New Age teaching, although New Agers usually draw from Eastern mysticism, rather than from the biblical texts quoted in *Science and Health*.

More recently, Lawrence LeShan, in his landmark book *The Medium, the Mystic, and the Physical*, outlined the distinctions between "Sensory Reality," the world we deal with every day, and the "Clairvoyant Reality." According to LeShan, mediums and psychics regularly experience Clairvoyant Reality, in which our own individual identity is an illusion.

After studying hundreds of psychic healing accounts, LeShan found a common thread: In most of the healings, the healer entered an altered state of consciousness, in which he or she perceived the unity of the patient with the universe. Somehow this perception conferred a benefit upon the healee. LeShan taught himself and others to enter this state, obtaining variable results but a clear New Age message: Healing is produced when we radically change the way we perceive ourselves.

Man Needs Enlightenment, not Redemption

According to New Agers, suffering of any kind arises from a lack of understanding of our perfection, not from rebellion against our Creator. As a result, we can be healed of disease and achieve wellness of body, mind, and spirit when we "get the picture" of our true identity.

So how do we "get the picture"? Holistic medicine offers a variety of methods, but perhaps the most popular is meditation. People are usually introduced to meditation as a simple, inexpensive technique for reducing stress, lowering blood pressure, and unleashing creative thinking.

Transcendental Meditation (TM) became popular in the 1970s by promoting such practical applications of meditation and camouflaging its underpinnings. Indeed, TM is one of the few holistic therapies mentioned in some medical textbooks. Similarly, Yoga has been promoted widely as a way to improve flexibility, muscle tone, and respiratory function.

Yet underneath the surface, meditation and Yoga have more profound intentions than improving muscle tone or reducing stress. They are designed to lead to an alteration of our worldview. A detailed review of the varieties of Yoga and meditation is impossible in this chapter, but three common characteristics of the "enlightenment" they produce are worth noting:

1. Normal, analytical thinking, or reflection for the purpose of gaining insight or understanding, is definitely not a goal. When the Psalms instruct us to meditate on the law of the Lord, they assume a meaningful flow of ideas, centered on a specific object. But in New Age meditation, a mantra—a word or phrase possessing some alleged power—is repeated over and over again, in order to short-circuit normal thinking.

2. Meditation leads to a "transcendence of the categories of good and evil." In one New Age anthology, Geoffrey Blundell states it plainly: "Meditation is only possible out of a silence in which evaluation and moral values have come to an end" (Blundell 1979, 197).

3. Both meditation and Yoga (which literally means *yoke* or *union*), if diligently pursued, lead to an experience of unity with all things and to personal divinity. In *The Holistic Health*

Handbook, psychologist Signy Knutsen writes, "The ultimate objective and effect of meditation. . . is a state of God-consciousness." Noting that while some meditators seek only a clear grasp of "All That Is," Knutsen declares that "others go beyond to seek identity or union with that One, that All-Pervading Reality, to realize again their Divinity" (Knutsen 1978, 256).

Enlightenment Leads to
Supernatural Paranormal Abilities

This New Age affirmation both attracts and repels potential recruits to the holistic movement. On one hand, some are intrigued by the possibility of developing special healing abilities that can be exercised without laborious analysis. Thousands of nurses, for example, have attended conferences to learn the technique of Therapeutic Touch. This form of laying on of hands, as taught by Dolores Krieger, Ph.D., involves a highly subjective "scanning" of invisible energy fields around the body, followed by a meditative infusion of *prana* (universal energy) into the patient.

On the other hand, some are turned off by holistic medicine's fascination with the paranormal—the psychics, shamans, spirit guides, and other apparent remnants of less scientific times. The movement is well endowed with case histories of healers: the "sleeping prophet," Edgar Cayce; the psychic surgeons of South America; American Indian shamans such as Rolling Thunder; even "respectable" psychics such as Olga Worrall. To New Agers, these people represent major contacts between our everyday world and realities beyond the five senses. As we evolve and transform ourselves, we are told, such break-throughs will become commonplace, and the barriers between science and religion will be dissolved.

All of the above presuppositions are clearly at odds with very basic biblical teaching, and yet many New Age therapies have made inroads into the Christian community. Proponents of "alternative" therapies in the Church argue that their techniques are natural workings of God's creation. They resent being labeled New Agers, yet may fail to see the spiritual implications of their work. Unfortunately, too few Christians understand the distinctions between biblical and New Age worldviews clearly enough to know what questions to ask. Indeed, if Christians cannot sort the wheat from the chaff in this area, we can expect little better from society at large.

As a step toward fostering discernment, here are some guidelines—some warnings—that may be of help in sizing up a particular therapy or health-care practitioner.

Beware of Psychic Diagnosis and Healing

The holistic-health movement, unlike conventional Western medicine, has shown intense interest in diagnoses arising from trance states, ESP, "spirit guides," out-of-body experiences, crystal gazing, aura reading, astrology, or the pendulum. These are the stock in trade of the old occult, supposedly tapping directly into a supernatural fund of knowledge. Likewise, New Age medicine has given credence to healings performed through incantations, psychic surgery, and channeling invisible energy.

Biblical teaching is quite clear and consistent about such things: "Let no one be found among you who . . . practices divination or sorcery, interprets omens, engages in witchcraft, or casts spells, or who is a medium or spiritist or who consults the dead. Anyone who does these things is detestable to the Lord . . ." (Deuteronomy 18:10–12).

We have been clearly warned not to deal with the supernatural, except in direct communication with God through prayer. Any other interactions are not only forbidden, but also frankly hazardous. We do not have to read far in Scripture to learn that the spiritual realm is not all sweetness and light. One-third of its inhabitants are described as powerful, cunning, and destructive. Tampering directly with their turf is about as intelligent as learning to swim in a lagoon full of great white sharks. Unfortunately, many assume that any event appearing supernatural must be from God. For them, a "miracle" serves as a gateway to dangerous deception.

Beware of Therapies Claiming to Manipulate "Life Energies"

Many of these therapies are based, at least in part, on Eastern mysticism or religious traditions with a monistic ("All Is One") worldview. For instance, Dolores Krieger's Therapeutic Touch is rooted in Vedantic Hinduism. Acupuncture and acupressure are firmly based in Taoism.

Some Christians feel they can use such therapies without buying into the philosophies behind them, claiming that a neutral phenomenon of God's creation has been misinterpreted by ancient mystics and New Agers. In light of the scarcity of evidence that these "life energies" actually exist, such a belief represents wishful thinking.

Questions or criticism are often deflected by a lame rationale: "I don't understand it; I just know it works." Unfortunately, those who feel they have been helped by an energy therapy are likely to be open to the New Age movement's explanations.

Beware of Therapies Grossly at Odds With Known Biological Mechanisms

Reflexology, for example, claims to treat ailing organs by massaging particular areas of the hand or foot. Iridology proposes that disease (past, present, and future) in all parts of the body is reflected by spots on the iris (the colored center of the eye).

The problem is that there is no basis in anatomy or physiology for either of those notions. In fact, one well-designed study at the University of California at San Diego showed that iridology was less able to identify patients with advanced kidney failure than random guessing (Simon, Worthen, and Mitas 1979, 1385–1389).

That brings up an important concept that is a corollary to the previous warning: Beware of systems that depend on testimonials to prove their validity.

We love testimonials, and we tend to believe in them. Most alternative therapies, and numerous nutrition/vitamin/weight-loss programs, depend almost entirely on anecdotes and testimonials from satisfied clients.

"I could never lose weight until I used . . ."

"Dr. Smith's acupressure treatments cleared up my back pain when nothing else worked."

"I've never felt better since I started taking . . ."

No doubt, those who gave the testimonials were sincere, but there may be a big gap between a personal experience and a logical cause-and-effect relationship that can be applied to the rest of humanity. Your back pain may seem to have improved after acupressure treatment, but it might be better because of an extra day's rest, the soothing voice of the therapist, the fact that touch feels good, or simply the fact that the body generally tends to heal itself. Even if the therapy worked for you, it does not mean that it would work for everyone else, or even for anyone else. What works for you may not work for me.

This may sound like coldhearted nitpicking, especially if you have been helped by a particular treatment. If you feel better, you probably couldn't care less about a scientific explanation. Unfortunately, improvement is not the only issue.

Human beings are very complex, and health and illness are affected by thousands of variables. For this reason, controlled studies are extremely important in determining whether a therapy is safe and effective. The long and laborious methods of Western medical research are not a clever scheme to keep alternative therapies out of the mainstream. They have evolved because it is so difficult to acquire reliable knowledge, and because reputable scientific institutions have a commitment (even if imperfectly kept) to protect people from worthless or harmful treatments.

I am not saying that science is the end all. Nor do I believe that we must subject Jesus' miracles, or even contemporary healings through prayer, to this same grinding process to prove that they happened. The scientific method assumes we are dealing with consistent, repeatable phenomena, not divine or demonic intervention. Miracles, by definition, do not lend themselves to controlled studies, but good observation can help assess how miraculous an event really is.

On the other hand, if a therapy is alleged to be a "natural part of God's creation," it should be open to study and criticism. Anyone who resists this study, especially while complaining that the medical establishment is trying to suppress them because of jealousy or greed, should be scrupulously avoided.

Beware of Therapists With Only One Answer

No construction worker tries to solve every problem with a hammer. Similarly, no one diet, one vitamin plan, one stress-reduction technique, or one therapy of any kind can deal effectively with every human disorder. While we all might wish for a simple cure-all for life's ills, good therapists will not use the same treatment on everyone who walks through the door. Neither will they make extravagant claims about their results or dodge legitimate questions.

Now that we have seen some general principles for discernment, we should take a look at a few therapies that have made inroads into both popular culture and the Christian community.

Acupuncture, Acupressure, and Applied Kinesiology

Ever since Western reporters in China were told of amazing cures and unexplainable anesthesia with needles, Americans have come to accept acupuncture as a legitimate therapy, if not their personal choice. The basic idea behind acupuncture is as follows:

In traditional Chinese medicine, the proper function of the body (not to mention the mind and spirit) hinges on the proper flow of "life energy," or Ch'i, through the body. Ch'i supposedly circulates through twelve pairs of invisible channels called meridians, most of which are identified with organs such as the liver and heart.

If the flow becomes sluggish or blocked, you might develop symptoms or overt disease. While the diagnosis is based partly on your history and general appearance, it depends most of all on the radial (wrist) pulses. With proper training (and much patience) the Chinese therapist can presumably assess all twelve meridians by feeling six positions at each wrist. If the flow of Ch'i needs to be improved, the therapist stimulates specific points on the skin, either by needling or by applying finger pressure.

Applied kinesiology (and some of its offshoots, such as behavioral kinesiology and Touch for Health), believes that the strength or weakness of certain muscle groups reflects the status of your internal organs, nutrition, emotional well-being, and even your spirituality. For example, a weak triceps muscle might indicate a problem in your pancreas, while the deltoid muscle (which helps raise the arm from the side) might indicate the condition of your gallbladder.

Frequently, certain foods or vitamins are held in one hand, or in the mouth, while the therapist tries to pull down the opposite, extended arm. If the arm weakens, the food is "toxic," or you are allergic to it. If the arm is stronger, you might benefit from the food. Entire dietary regimes are constructed from such testing. All of this is based on the idea that the flow of Ch'i somehow communicates the status of your far-flung internal organs through the various "indicator" muscles.

The basic tenets of the system are found in Chinese medicine's original text, *The Yellow Emperor's Classic of Internal Medicine,* which consists largely of long discourses on philosophy and Taoist metaphysics. According to historian Ilza Veith, who translated the work, this was "the only way in which early Chinese medical thinking could be expressed, for medicine was but a part of philosophy and religion, both of which propounded oneness with nature, i.e., the universe" (Veith 1966, 4).

The idea that Ch'i flows through your body in defined channels comes from Taoism, and it is now deeply tied, in contemporary New Age spirituality, to the belief that this universal energy is what Western religions have traditionally called God. Evarts Loomis, who pioneered in establishing holistic health centers, told one of the first large conferences in San Diego that "expanded consciousness depends upon the inflow of primal energies variously referred to by different cultures as the Logos, prana, Ch'i, Buddha, nature, the Word, the Holy Spirit, Cosmic energy, etc. Who can say that these words are not synonymous?" (Loomis 1977, 73.)

Some Christian practitioners who use these New Age techniques argue that they are simply making use of a neutral phenomenon (as electricity is neutral). They say the fact that we don't understand why something works shouldn't automatically consign a practice to the realm of the occult. Some even claim to have "recaptured" the techniques from the New Age camp, and thus put them to work for godly purposes. This is, unfortunately, easier said than proven, especially when the concept is a basic precept of a religious system.

Suppose, for instance, you assume that such a life energy exists, but instead of calling it Ch'i, you call it bioenergy, in order to divorce it from its Eastern mystical connotations. You still face a major problem. Over the past several decades, biologists and physiologists have failed to detect bioenergy. No structure, biochemical function, or electrical event in the body appears to correlate with it, even though the Chinese provided detailed maps to follow. (New Agers often display as proof Kirlian photography, which shows some eerie emanations from hands or other objects. But there is no visible order to the emanations to support the detailed charts in Chinese medicine.)

Somehow, this energy that no one can measure is supposed to cause major changes in muscle strength and general health. The claims and the evidence simply don't match.

Homeopathy

This practice, whose name literally means "same disease," predates the holistic-health movement by one-hundred-fifty years, but current interest in drugless therapy has given it an unexpected surge of popularity.

In 1810, German physician Samuel Hahnemann published *Organon of Medicine*, in which he set forth the principles of a new healing system. In essence, he concluded that "like cures like." In other words, the best remedy for a disorder is a substance that causes the same symptoms in a healthy person.

In order to prevent unpleasant side effects, Hahnemann diluted his medicines, first by factors of one-tenth or one-hundredth, and later by astronomical proportions. The efficacy of the substance, even in such infinitesimal concentrations, was said to be maintained (in fact, enhanced) by a process of vigorous shaking at each step of dilution.

What was the basis for the apparent cures resulting from homeopathic treatment? According to George Vithoulkas, author of two textbooks on homeopathy, greatly diluted remedies "contained no detectable material trace of the original substance. It followed, therefore, that their curative effect was not material, but involved some other factor—energy. . . . Hahnemann concluded that [illness] was nothing other than a derangement in the life force of man" (Vithoulkas 1978, 89).

Not all homeopaths consider the extreme dilutions central to their practice. But this life-force theory of homeopathy, in which an undetectable substance has a profound influence on an unmeasurable energy, has been stressed in the holistic health movement. That homeopathy would be virtually ignored by the scientific mainstream should come as no great surprise; contemporary health studies are usually designed around theories that have some basis in the prevailing body of biological knowledge.

One of homeopathy's weaknesses is that it stands or falls on the "like cures like" principle. While this may appear true when you look at the side effects of certain medicines, it is too simplistic a framework upon which to hang a comprehensive health-care program. If homeopathy is ever to gain serious recognition in the scientific community, its proponents must bring forth some reasonably controlled studies that demonstrate their remedies relieve symptoms or reverse pathology more effectively than a placebo. (Such studies may indeed exist, but if so, they have not been widely disseminated.)

Otherwise, business as usual will continue. Homeopathic physicians will practice with the dedication they have maintained since the days of Hahnemann, but they will remain isolated from the scientific community. And New Agers will continue to use homeopathy's extreme dilutions as an illustration of the role of "life energy" in the body.

Biofeedback

This therapy has generated some controversy among Christians who study the New Age movement. Basically, biofeedback refers to any treatment that gives (or feeds back to) the patient information about body functions he normally does not perceive or control. Such functions include heart rate, blood pressure, skin temperature, muscle tightness, and EEG waves. The object is to gain control over an automatic function.

The question is whether such control is a valid tool to relieve suffering, or a passport to the occult. You can look at it either way.

An example of a positive use for biofeedback is in the control of migraine headaches. Migraines occur when an artery in the head spontaneously contracts, thus reducing the blood supply to a localized area of the brain. This may produce visual flashes of light or more severe symptoms, such as transient paralysis.

Usually, the same artery then dilates, causing a severe, pounding headache.

Migraine headaches are usually treated by medication that either attempts to prevent the initial contraction, block the subsequent dilation, or smother the pain. But biofeedback therapists have found that migraine sufferers who learn to control the skin temperature in their hands (which is a direct function of small-artery diameter) are often able to abort their headaches. Certainly, a drugless approach to migraine headaches would be more desirable than using medications that may have troublesome side effects.

On the surface, it is hard to object to this application of biofeedback. It is based on known physiology, involves no mystical energies, and does not require a worldview transplant. Some might argue that we weren't meant to control skin temperature, but similar statements were once made about airplanes and our lack of wings.

Those who object to biofeedback point out that many biofeedback therapists, including pioneer researchers Elmer and Alyce Green, have been heavily involved in efforts to induce altered states of consciousness and psychic abilities by using biofeedback as a sort of high-tech Yoga. As a result, some Christians have felt biofeedback should be avoided altogether.

While acknowledging that this technology is certainly misused, it seems to me that biofeedback can be an appropriate tool for managing certain physiological disorders. To dismiss it because of the bad company it has kept is like condemning all movies (even those with a Christian message) because many movies convey negative values.

If a patient can use biofeedback to learn how to stop or reduce headaches, relieve muscle tension, or lower blood pressure—without becoming involved in various altered states of consciousness—this technique can serve a useful purpose. Needless to say, it is important to use caution in choosing a biofeedback therapist.

There are a number of other therapies in the holistic medical bag, far too many to review in this chapter. Ultimately it is more important to develop a clearly defined, biblically based world-view than to rely on a predigested list of do's and don'ts regarding unfamiliar practices. A well-developed Christian perspective, combined with a basic understanding of New Age thinking, will help stem a very attractive but dangerous tide.

4

SCIENCE: QUANTUM PHYSICS AND QUANTUM LEAPS

Dean C. Halverson

WATCH OUT FOR SCIENTIFIC EXPLOSIONS. THEY ARE ALMOST CERTAIN TO entail major fallout upon religion. Back in the early 1600s, Galileo came up with his theory that the planets, including the earth, revolved around the sun. Before long, people were questioning the authority of the Roman Catholic Church. In the 1800s, Charles Darwin developed his theory of evolution. Before long, people were questioning the existence of God.

Although you may not be aware of it, another scientific explosion rocked the world in the early 1900s. Between 1900 and 1930, Einstein changed our view of absolute time and space by showing how time and space are related to each other, to energy, to gravity, and to the speed of light. While Einstein dealt with the very large—the cosmos—other physicists began experimenting with the very small—subatomic particles. Their research became known as quantum mechanics, or quantum physics. The term *quanta* refers to the units of energy discontinuously absorbed and radiated by subatomic particles. Together, Einstein's relativity theories and quantum mechanics are referred to as the "new physics."

According to New Age writers, the new physics, especially quantum physics, supports their new worldview. They point out how the writings of the new physicists parallel those of the Eastern mystics. For example, Michael Talbot writes, in *Mysticism and the New Physics:* "It is what the mystics have been telling us all along. This, then, is the guiding topic of this book—to point out the confluence of mysticism and the new physics" (Talbot 1981, 4, 5).

Gary Zukav, in *The Dancing Wu Li Masters,* speaks of "those similarities between Eastern philosophies and physics that seemed to me so obvious and significant" (Zukav 1979, 26). And Fritjof Capra, whose first book, *The Tao of Physics,* has sold over a half million copies, writes, "The concepts of modern physics often show surprising parallels to the ideas expressed in the religious philosophies of the Far East" (Capra 1975, 17, 18).

Marilyn Ferguson also claims scientific support for the mystical worldview: "Science is only now verifying what humankind has known intuitively since the dawn of history" (Ferguson 1980, 151).

But such claims raise a number of questions about the relationship between science and religion: What are the limits of science? What can science tell us about the identity of God? Has quantum physics really changed science that much? And what is the religious fallout from this latest scientific explosion?

In the West, we have traditionally believed that science deals with objective reality and religion deals with an objective, personal God. In the minds of the New Agers, however, both science and religion have become much more subjective.

Quantum Mechanics: A Revolution in Physics

Before 1900, classical physicists compared the universe to a machine. Like a machine, it was viewed as determined and predictable. All things related to one another in a cause-and-effect relationship. If you wanted to understand how something worked, you broke it down into its constituent parts.

Our machinelike universe was also objective. Scientists assumed that it could be observed without the observation causing any significant change to it. Although classical physicists were unable to explore the submicroscopic realm, they assumed the same ground rules applied to it as applied to the macroscopic realm.

But as scientists began exploring the atomic realm through new technology, they found something quite surprising. No longer could reality be compared to a machine; now it was something quite mysterious.

Enter quantum mechanics.

To understand quantum mechanics or quantum physics, you need to understand two principles and something called "the measurement problem."

The first principle, called the Principle of Complementarity, was formulated by Danish physicist Niels Bohr. When physicists discovered the parts of the atom—electrons, protons, and neutrons—they discovered those parts sometimes behaved like waves and sometimes like particles. That didn't make sense to them; it was difficult to fathom. Bohr concluded that instead of questioning what seemed to be the paradoxical nature of the subatomic realm, he had to accept it, and that's what his Principle of Complementarity is about. It states that although a subatomic particle exhibits mutually exclusive characteristics, both aspects must be taken into account in order to get the whole picture. In other words, if you want to understand an electron, you have to look at it holistically, instead of trying to break it down reductionalistically.

Werner Heisenberg, a onetime Bohr colleague, later discovered another complementary relationship in addition to wave/particle duality. Sometimes subatomic particles reacted like solid bits of matter. At other times, they seemed to act more like forms of energy. To describe what was happening, he wrote of a relationship known as the Uncertainty Principle (Heisenberg 1958).

As benign as Heisenberg's Uncertainty Principle seems, it changed the nature of physics. In a science based on predictability, the Uncertainty Principle said that fundamental reality was unpredictable. Not only was the concept of predictability eroded, but so was objectivity, another foundation of classical physics.

The quantum realm didn't seem to be playing by the rules.

In the macroscopic realm, you can predict the outcome of a single event because all the involved forces are discoverable. In the quantum realm, however, not all the forces are discoverable, so you have to work with the statistical percentages of an ensemble of events. In other words, you can predict only the probability of a certain result. That's where "the measurement problem" comes in. Simply stated, the measurement problem asks: What causes the quantum realm to move from a state of possibility to a state of actuality? Frankly, the measurement problem is still controversial. Einstein felt our knowledge about the quantum realm was incomplete, but that after more experimentation, we would eventually discover the laws of that realm and its hidden variables. However, physicist C. F. von Weizsacker felt that the mysteries of the quantum realm would never be discovered. Quantum reality, he said, is so unlike the reality with which we are familiar that it is unimaginable. Still another physicist, Heisenberg, said that quantum reality is run by chance, rather than by determinate laws.

No matter whose opinion you adopt, you have to admit that quantum physics has drastically changed the way physicists view the nature of reality.

According to many physicists today, fundamental reality appears to behave paradoxically, to be run by chance, and to require holistic, rather than reductionistic, understanding. Besides that, quantum physics has also broken down the imaginary barrier that stood between the subject and the object. The influence of the act of observation must now be considered. No longer can the scientist be viewed as a dispassionate observer; now he is an active participant.

What is happening in science parallels what is happening in religion. Just as quantum physics has affected the idea of a strictly separate, objective reality in science, so Eastern mysticism has changed the minds of many regarding an objective, personal God. As both science and religion have become more subjective, the New Agers have merged the two views of reality into one.

Transformation: The New Hope

New Agers point out that our culture is facing many crises: social, economic, international, ecological, and so on. Everywhere you turn, it seems you bump into a major crisis. Why do we have so many major crises today? The answer, according to New Agers, is simple: Because we have an outdated, reductionistic worldview.

How can we cope? How can we confront these crises? That, too, is simple, say the New Agers. What we need is both a personal and a social transformation. *Transformation* is the key word. It is a central theme of the New Age movement. In fact, the subtitle to Ferguson's *The Aquarian Conspiracy* is *Personal and Social Transformation in the 1980s.* Another New Age book, *Changing Images of Man,* promotes a worldview called "evolutionary transformationalism."

But how do we experience transformation? It comes, say the New Agers, as we change the image we have of ourselves and of reality.

Peter Russell says we need to move away from an individualistic image, which causes possessiveness and alienation, to an image of oneness. The new image of oneness, says Russell, will change behavior from selfishness to love for others and for nature (Russell 1983, 155).

When you see yourself as one with the rest of creation, you will love your neighbor as yourself, and you will also love nature as yourself. In *The Turning Point*, Capra (1975, 412) calls this image of oneness "deep ecology."

> Deep ecology is supported by modern science . . . but it is rooted in a perception of reality that goes beyond the scientific framework to an intuitive awareness of all life, the interdependence of its multiple manifestations and its cycles of change and transformation. When the concept of the human spirit is understood in this sense, as the mode of consciousness in which the individual feels connected to the cosmos as a whole, it becomes clear that ecological awareness is truly spiritual.

So Capra says that spirituality is a mode of consciousness, and the goal of this mode of consciousness is to feel connected to the cosmos as a whole. Capra's thought progression is subtle but significant, because it represents how New Agers view religion. According to New Agers, the essence of religion is consciousness. The end result of that consciousness is a feeling of oneness with the cosmos. The inevitable implication that follows from this train of thought is that the cosmos is also a form of consciousness.

For the New Ager, the identification of the cosmos with consciousness links science to religion. Thus Capra can write, "The scientists and the mystics . . . have developed highly sophisticated methods of observing nature. . . . Both are records of inquiries into the nature of the universe" (Capra 1975, 36).

Dynamic Oneness: The New God

In 1972, George Leonard wrote that "a first step in the Transformation" is to have a "sense of oneness with all existence" (24).

79

Physicist Capra argues that oneness, or interconnectedness, is the only way to make sense of the entire universe: "A careful analysis of the process of observation in atomic physics shows that the subatomic particles have no meaning as isolated entities but can be understood only as interconnections, or correlations, between various processes of observation and measurement" (Capra 1982, 80). He then states, "This is how modern physics reveals the basic oneness of the universe. It shows that we cannot decompose the world into independently existing smallest units" (80, 81). In another place, he writes, "In quantum theory you never end up with things, you always deal with interconnections" (80).

Like Capra, Ferguson places great importance on interrelatedness: "When things come together something new happens. In relationship there is novelty, creativity, richer complexity.... Modern science has verified the quality of whole-making, the characteristic of nature to put things together in an ever-more synergistic, meaningful pattern" (Ferguson 1980, 156).

When Ferguson combines the idea of organizational dynamism with the theory of evolution, suddenly the world itself contains inner purpose and direction. "These wholes—in effect, these unions—are dynamic, evolutionary, creative," she writes. "They thrust toward ever-higher orders of complexity and integration" (Ferguson 1980, 156).

Interestingly, the concepts of interrelated wholeness and organizational dynamism come together in Ferguson's definition of God:

> In the emergent spiritual tradition God is not the personage of our Sunday-school mentality.... God is experienced as flow, wholeness, the infinite kaleidoscope of life and death, Ultimate Cause, the ground of being.... God is the consciousness that manifests as lila, the play of the universe (Ferguson, 1980, 382).

Reality Structurer: The New Person

Not only do New Agers say that all things are interrelated and all things are one, but they also emphasize that the barrier between the observer and the observed is broken down. The object is interrelated to the observer. To put it in Zukav's words, "At the subatomic level, we cannot observe something without changing it" (Zukav 1979, 134).

Capra goes even further: "The electron does not have objective properties independent of my mind"(Capra 1982, 87). And Talbot says it this way: "The entire physical universe itself is nothing more than patterns of neuronal energy firing off inside our heads" (Talbot 1981, 54). Our consciousness, according to the New Agers, forms and creates reality. Talbot concludes that "there is no physical world 'out there.' Consciousness creates all," and that "Our consciousness is all-powerful" (Talbot 1981, 152).

You see what I mean. If the New Agers are right regarding the implications of quantum physics on religion, then all previous scientific revolutions were insignificant, compared with this one. Before, some scientists claimed that science made the idea of a Creator-God obsolete, but now the New Agers claim science shows not only that an objective, personal God is not necessary, but also that we ourselves create reality.

What is reality, then? The stuff of reality, according to New Agers, is mind—or consciousness. Again we see how New Agers have merged science with religion. To them, both science and religion deal with the nature of ultimate reality, which they say is consciousness.

The New Age emphasis on consciousness as being the "stuff" of reality affects their view of what constitute legitimate areas for scientific research. For instance, the New Age movement is striving to make psychic research, or parapsychology, an acceptable area of scientific research. Edgar D. Mitchell, a former Apollo astronaut, is a prime example of a scientist who is convinced of the value of researching the power of the consciousness through psychic phenomena such as clairvoyance and telekinesis. He writes, "Psychic research is perhaps the primary area from which the [scientific] revolution will come and from which a new paradigm of science will be constructed" (Mitchell 1974, 44).

Subjective Idealism: The Breakdown of Science

The New Agers say that because the nature of reality is consciousness, our minds are able to construct reality. If a person cannot observe a quantum particle without changing the particle's state, the mind of the observer directly influences the state of the quantum realm.

New Agers are certainly correct when they say that we influence the quantum realm to some extent whenever we observe it, yet the influence is an indirect one. We don't influence the quantum realm by our minds, but by our means of observation.

Ian Barbour, author of *Issues in Science and Religion*, says it well: "It is the detection apparatus, not the observer as a human being, which influences the measurement obtained" (Barbour 1971, 287). When he speaks of the detection apparatus, he is referring to such measuring devices as clocks, meter sticks, photographic plates—not minds or people. In other words, we must understand the difference between the physical act of measurement, which includes the measuring apparatus, and the psychical act of measurement, which includes the human observer. Heisenberg himself made such a distinction.

What is at issue here is the question of an objective reality. If you cannot assume that reality is to some extent independent of observation, then science is not possible, because my description of the results of an experiment would say nothing about what may have happened in your reality.

Dr. Richard Bube, professor of materials science and electrical engineering at Stanford University, writes: "Authentic science is unreservedly committed to the existence of an objective reality . . . Our knowledge of this reality must indeed be personal knowledge, but this does not imply that it is therefore subjective knowledge" (Bube 1982, 10–13).

This is a distinction made by the new physics, but not by the New Agers. The new physics theory grants that our knowledge is personal and does influence the quantum realm, but it does not deny the objective existence of that realm.

A scientist must believe in objective reality, but New Agers say that reality is based on subjective knowledge. That makes it very curious when New Age authors claim scientific support for their worldview, since that worldview claims science has no validity. It is also curious that they claim scientific support for a view saying the mind creates material reality, even though science says the physical universe existed long before anybody was around to observe it.

Even physicist David Bohm, whose writings many New Agers claim as support for their ideas, says:

> Indeed this [idea of the centrality of the mind] is often carried to such an extreme that it appears as if nothing ever happens without the observer. However, we know of many physical processes, even at the level of quantum phenomena, that do occur without any direct intervention of the observer. Take, for example, the processes that go on in a distant star. These appear to follow the known laws of physics and the processes occur, and have occurred, without any significant intervention on our part (Wilber 1983, 145, 146).

One such demonstration is the consistency of the quantum realm. No matter who observes it, its behavior is consistent. Although you cannot predict the outcome of a single event in the quantum realm, you can statistically calculate the percentage of what does occur. For example, after you shoot one hundred particles of light at a screen, you might observe that ten percent of those particles hit in one area and ninety percent in another area. That same percentage will occur no matter how often the experiment is repeated and no matter who is doing the observing.

The New Age assumption that ultimate reality is an impersonal consciousness cannot account for the consistency we observe in the quantum realm. If, on the other hand, ultimate reality (God) is personal, we can easily explain this consistency. We are not responsible for the formation of reality; God is. The existence of a personal God not only explains consistency, but also explains the objectivity we sense in reality—the objectivity that is necessary in order to explore science.

The Limits of Science and Religion

When New Agers minimize the distinction between mind and matter, subject and object, they also lose the distinction between the natural and the supernatural. That is why New Agers identify science with religion. In their minds, both physicists and mystics deal with ultimate reality.

That, however, is an unproven assumption. Even if physicists have uncovered a basic oneness in the universe and mystics have experienced a universal oneness, it is not necessarily true that either are dealing with ultimate reality. More likely, they are dealing with a lower level of reality, rather than a higher one: a subscendence, not a transcendence.

Christians and New Agers alike would do well to realize that science is fickle. Many people believe science is the final answer, but science changes. If we attach our religious beliefs too closely to science, then those beliefs will collapse the next time science changes.

Ian Barbour gives a healthy perspective on the limitations of science (Barbour 1971, 289, 290):

> The primary significance of modern physics lies not in any disclosure of the fundamental nature of reality, but in the recognition of the limitations of science. . . . The contemporary scientist is aware that any theory is partial, tentative and incomplete. Hu-

mility and caution in extending a particular theory into a total philosophy of life are more prevalent. . . . Neither classical nor modern physics—nor any other specialized science—can do justice to all aspects of human experience or provide a comprehensive world-view. The most we should expect from physics is a modest contribution to a view of nature at one limited level.

Barbour mentions two points that deserve further attention. His first point deals with level confusion and can be illustrated by brain researcher Donald MacKay's analogy of a neon sign (MacKay 1974, 37). On one level, the neon sign is merely a collection of wires, glass tubes, electrodes, and gases. If you approach the sign on the level of the technician, you will get a good understanding of the physical mechanisms of the sign and how they function. You might even be able to repair the sign when it breaks down. But no matter how complete a description the technician might give from his or her perspective, that description would not explain other levels of meaning. For example, the technician's approach could not interpret the message of the sign. In order to understand what the sign said, you would need to approach it from the perspective of the linguist.

To say that the technician's perspective does not explain the message of the sign does not mean that the technician's explanation was incomplete on its particular level. The technician's description may have been very complete. Nor is it true that the completeness of the technician's description of the sign negates the linguist's description.

The point is that reality can be viewed from several levels, and each level has its own limitations, as well as its own terminology.

To say that science has its limitations does not mean it is limited in its territory of research, but rather that it is limited in its methods. Because of the nature of the scientific method—its rationality, its emphasis on empirical observation, repeatability, and testability, and its demand for publicly observable data—science is not qualified to address certain subjects. For example, science can explain the mechanics of an abortion, but it cannot provide moral guidelines for abortions.

New Agers, on the other hand, believe science is now able to address the ultimate questions. Paul Davies reflects that attitude in *God and the New Physics:* "Deep questions of existence . . . are not new. What is new is that we may at last be on the verge of answering them. This astonishing prospect stems from some spectacular recent advances in physical science—not only the new physics, but its close relative, the new cosmology." Then Davies adds, "Science offers a surer path to God than religion" (Davies 1983, vii–viii).

New Agers have not married science and religion; they have redefined them. Their redefinitions, however, do not do justice to either one. For instance, their idealistic view of reality, in which objective reality is formed by the organizational abilities of the individual mind, makes science impossible. In a similar way, their redefinition of religion is inadequate to explain all aspects of reality.

This brings us to Barbour's second point: The limitations of science. Science is able to explain the workings of physical reality, but it is not adequate, nor was it ever intended, to explain all of reality.

Religion is different from science in that it must be adequate to explain all of reality. By relegating God to the position of an impersonal force acting within the universe, New Agers have diminished God to one aspect of reality. The God of the New Agers, however, cannot account for the value of personhood, the meaning of history, or the presence of conscience.

Scientist Paul Davies, whose concept of God is quite similar to that of the New Agers' concept of the organizing principle, faces the same problems. Although he concludes that the existence of the universe can be explained by a natural, rather than supernatural, God—a kind of supermind working within the universe—he has to admit that his god cannot deal with key aspects of existence, "for example, purpose or morality." He says (Davies 1983, 227, 228): "I am sometimes asked whether the insight which physicists have gained into the workings of nature through the study of fundamental processes throws any light on the nature of God's plan for the universe, or reveals the struggle between good and evil. It does not." Neither does the god of the New Agers.

In *The Global Brain* (1983), author Peter Russell says that if we just expand our awareness beyond our "skin-encapsulated ego" and sense the oneness of all things, we will feel a great bond of love for one another. But is the sharing of a common consciousness sufficient motivation to curb our sinful nature? It is true that unless I feel I am valuable and loved, I will not view others as valuable and I will not have the ability to love them. But does the feeling of divine oneness give me sufficient grounds for value and love? It is meaningless to say the impersonal ground of being is loving, because love is something that happens between persons, not between an impersonal oneness and a person. Only a personal God provides sufficient grounds for love and value.

God Upholding Creation

According to the Bible, there is a relationship between God and the universe. The first words of Scripture address that relationship: "In the beginning God created the heavens and the earth" (Genesis 1:1).

God, who has always existed, is the One who brought the universe into existence. Although God depends upon no one outside Himself for His existence, the universe depends upon God for its existence. To use a New Age expression, God brought the universe into actuality.

Although the Bible teaches the transcendence of God, in that God is radically other than His creation, the Bible also teaches the immanence of God, in that He is very close to His creatures (see Acts 17:27, 28). The immanence of God is shown by the fact that God not only created the universe but continues to uphold it (*see* Colossians 1:17; Hebrews 1:3).

Because God upholds the universe, the universe reflects the nature of God (*see* Psalms 19:1; Romans 1:20). According to the Bible, the universe reflects God's nature, but it never becomes His nature.

MacKay puts it this way (1974, 59):

> Imagine a TV screen which an artist could use as a medium; a human artist who, instead of laying down paint on canvas with a brush, lays down a continual pattern of events on a screen, with the aid of some flexible electronic contraption.
>
> Imagine now a scene brought into being by our artist, in which . . . a cricket match is taking place. If the artist is good at his job, then we, as we watch it, will see a coherent sequence of events: the ball moving through the air in a nearly parabolic arc, and so forth. We will be able, at least in principle, to discover for ourselves some of the laws of motion and laws of behavior of the world that our artist has invented—or shall we say created.

MacKay's analogy has its limitations, but it does illustrate God's relationship to the world. Although the act of observation does affect the universe, as quantum physics says, the universe does not depend on our observation for its existence. Reality exhibits an objectivity because its existence depends on something other than us: God. A personal, transcendent God makes science possible. Through scientific techniques, we are able to discover laws in the universe—not because we mentally invent them, but because the Creator placed them there. They are a reflection of His coherence, not ours.

The concepts of the New Agers may be adequate to explain the organization of the universe. But if you wish to explain the value of personhood and the meaning of morality, then the New Ager's view of God as an impersonal organizing principle falls short. If creation reflects the nature of the Creator at all, then God must be supremely personal, not impersonal.

The Challenge to Autonomy

What is the consequence of the New Agers' thinking? What is the logical result of viewing God as an impersonal force? There are several answers.

When we deny God's personhood, the sense of God being other than us diminishes. God becomes a mystical being who is part of all existence. Without a transcendent God to sustain the value of separate objects in an objective reality, reality collapses into a oneness. God becomes identified with the mystical oneness, even as we are; thus we become divine.

More and more, we become the primary object of study, and we lose accountability to anything or anyone outside ourselves. We become radically autonomous. We become the sole source of meaning, truth, and value. We take on the ability to create and control our own reality. In short, we take on the attributes of God.

The Bible says that the desire to usurp the position and authority of God and relegate Him to a place where He is manageable is an inherent human inclination. It is part of our sinful nature. Because of that sinful inclination, we are not able to discover the true God on our own.

Although New Agers assume that they have an inherent ability to know God, the Bible says the human bent toward sin drastically influences our perception of who God is. We automatically make God into an image with which we are comfortable.

If God were an organizational force, then we could discover Him through science. If God were the oneness of consciousness, then we could experience Him through mysticism. But if God is a person, then neither science nor mysticism is adequate to discover His mysteries.

Scientist C. A. Coulson puts it this way (1955, 90):

If we think for a moment of our friends, then ...
the scientific method may be applied to them: they
may be described in psychological terms and they
may be systematized and scheduled in biochemical
language so that in one sense we know all about
them. But in another, and deeper sense, we shall
then know nothing. Our examination will have
thrown light on the nature of scientific thinking; it is
most unlikely that it will have said very much about
our friends.

When writing about God, the apostle John used the term
logos ("word"), which the Greeks used to refer to the universal
reason that permeated the world. The Greeks used the word
logos in a way similar to the New Age idea of an organizational
dynamism. By force of his experience with Jesus Christ, however, John changed the meaning of *logos* to refer to a person,
rather than to an impersonal organizational principle. Moreover, this Word, who John said was God, the Creator of all
things, became one of us.

If God is indeed personal, which is what best fits the
evidence around us, then, as with any person, we can know
Him only if He decides to reveal Himself to us. Neither science
nor mysticism can lead us to an intimate knowledge of the
person of God. The good news is that God was willing to reveal
Himself to us through the person of His Son, Jesus Christ, the
Word made flesh, "Through [whom] all things were made"
(John 1:3).

5

POLITICS: BUILDING AN INTERNATIONAL PLATFORM

Douglas R. Groothuis

IDEAS HAVE POLITICAL CONSEQUENCES, AND THAT INCLUDES RELIGIOUS ideas. In fact, politics frequently walks in the footsteps of faith. Since the root idea of New Agers' faith is Oneness—Oneness with nature and Oneness within the human race—it is logical for their political priorities to concern ecology, sexual equality, and world order (or unification).

Regarding ecology, physicist Fritjof Capra argues that we must enter the solar age and stop depending on fossil fuels (1982). In his book *New Age Politics*, political visionary Mark Satin outlines several strategies to switch from nuclear power and nonrenewable energy sources to other sources. He calls for the White House to convert to passive solar energy (Satin 1978).

Regarding sexual equality, Capra believes that culture is shifting from a patriarchy to a balance, or a combination of the yin (feminine) and yang (masculine) elements of traditional Taoism. The West's suppression of the yin has led to an exploitative and rationalistic culture (Capra 1982). Starhawk, a neo-pagan follower of the great goddess, rejects patriarchal religion and politics and any nation of justice fixed in external deity, for "we must create justice and ecological and social balance; this is the prime concern . . . of ethics in a worldview that sees deity as immanent in human life and the world" (Spretnak 1982, 421). For many New Agers, the new politics includes the supposed right of women to "control their own bodies" through abortion on demand.

Simply put, New Agers believe we are gods and our collective divinity demands political responsibility. The earth goddess must awaken in us all, so we can connect again with the One. The prevailing order oppresses women in the name of a male deity. To free women, the Christian God must be usurped by the collective divinity rediscovered within. Yet the "goddess" (or Gaia) is but a religious symbol, not a *personal* being like the God of the Bible.

World Order

Since cosmic consciousness knows all as One, New Age political consciousness sees the world as one interlocking, interpenetrating system. Therefore, national boundaries and divisions must be transcended, for we all share a cosmic humanity that must become political. Newtonian politics fragmented the world into isolated and independent nation-states, just as Newtonian physics broke the physical world into separate, independent shards. While we often view patriotism or national sovereignty as virtues, New Agers say they promote separation and exclusivity.

The New Age claims that the world of monistic religions, modern psychology, and new physics seeks merger. According to New Agers, we must view all as vital parts of one planet. The New Age worldview dissolves all boundaries between God and humanity, humans and other humans, or humans and nature.

All is One. Moreover, since mobility and communication have unified the world technologically, peoples who once were culturally and geographically isolated can now be linked. As Mark Satin remarks (1978, 142):

> The destiny of mankind, after its long preparatory period of separation and differentiation, is at last to become one ... This unity is on the point of being politically expressed in a world government that will unite nations and regions in transactions beyond their individual capacity.

New Age politics projects a political order in tune with the cosmic order. "Planetary consciousness," Satin says, "recognizes our oneness with all humanity and in fact with all life, everywhere, and with the planet as a whole" (1978, 148).

Under this New Age agenda, nations are united into a new political and economic order, to redress the imbalance of prosperity and peace. Likewise, the new global society must disarm itself of nuclear weapons, to live as one in peace.

Satin speaks of a planetary guidance system that would avoid the rigidities of a one-world government and regulate world culture without organizing it. For instance, he offers a system of planetary taxation (imagine deciphering *that* tax form) on resource use that would help redistribute wealth to poorer nations. Although they promote a vision of planetary unity, Satin, Marilyn Ferguson, and others also claim to support a decentralized civil government. Government must be reduced to a more manageable, human scale. How they reconcile their view of a unified world order and a decentralized civil government is not always clear.

Putting the One to Work

Satin's ideas are not simply idle theory. Many organizations are energetically working to see them established as reality.

One such group is Planetary Citizens. Founded in 1972 by

Donald Keys, a longtime consultant to the United Nations, Planetary Citizens has attracted such New Age luminaries as David Spangler and Peter Caddy (both formerly of the Findhorn community), William Irwin Thompson, futurist Willis Harman, former astronaut Edgar Mitchell, and Michael Murphy (of Esalen Institute). Distinguished members include Isaac Asimov, Rene Dubos, and honorary chairman Norman Cousins.

Humanity, says Keys, is evolving toward Omega, or unification of consciousness and culture. Keys says that New Consciousness communities like Findhorn and growth centers like Esalen will lead the passage to planetization and will provide the "myths which will form and inform the emergent world order" (Keys 1982, 72). According to Keys, the flagship for planetization is the United Nations.

In early 1982, Planetary Citizens and several other groups kicked off a consciousness-raising project called Planetary Initiative for the World We Choose. For Keys, it was a coming-out party for the politically disorganized New Age. Study groups were formed; a newspaper, the *Initiator*, was published; and much attention was attracted. It all culminated in a Planetary Congress in Toronto, in June of 1983. Nearly five hundred people, including New Age notables Barbara Marx Hubbard and Ram Dass, met with people from twenty countries during the four-day event.

The "Declaration on the World We Choose," drafted by the congress and published in the *Initiator* (September 1983), reveals its New Age orientation on ecology, economics, politics, and other topics. It also affirms the pivotal need to achieve "the individual human potential and ... the essential spiritual identity of each person, giving rise to a oneness with all life." It also trumpets the need for a new economic order, a stronger United Nations, and a centralized global government.

According to Keys, we are "already in the midst of the final planetary revolution" where "human consciousness is moving on to become a continuous, non-segmented medium" that will "become the normal moral medium for the new politics of the planet" (Keys 1982, 102).

If there are any doubts about Keys' political and spiritual agenda, look at his book *Earth at Omega*. It is dedicated to Sri Chinmoy, Hindu guru and United Nations chaplain, and to Djwhal Khul, a Tibetan spiritual adept who supposedly telepathically inspired theosophist Alice Bailey in her writings on occultism, world government, and world religion.

Another political lobby, World Goodwill, is more directly led by Alice Bailey's teachings. Like Planetary Citizens, it is headquartered at the United Nations Plaza. Its purpose is to unfold "the Plan" as spelled out in Bailey's *The Externalization of the Hierarchy* (Bailey 1975). Along with her other works, Bailey claims this one was telepathically received from Djwhal Khul, who predicted the galvanization of a new world government and world religion by "the Christ," an advanced member of a spiritual hierarchy whose emergence is summoned by invoking a prayer ("The Great Invocation") widely distributed by Bailey's followers.

Bailey taught that the New Age will dawn after a global crisis that only "the Christ" (not Jesus Christ) would rectify. But if we offset our present futility and frustration, we can build a new world through belief in our divinity. A new world will result—one that will eclipse traditional Christianity.

World Goodwill is merely one of several Bailey-oriented groups sponsored by Lucis Trust. Originally Lucifer Trust, this occult organization came about when Bailey broke from Theosophy.

In recent years, one of Bailey's disciples, Benjamin Creme, has heralded the imminent reappearance of Bailey's "Christ," or Maitreya (Creme 1980). Claiming to be telepathically "overshadowed" by the "Christ," Creme transmits "Maitreyan" talks on spirituality and politics.

Early in the 1980s, Creme organized a global advertising campaign to announce Maitreya's advent and to invoke him through The Great Invocation. The ads in major newspapers also promised that Maitreya would end world hunger, war, and strife and would usher in a one-world socialist government that would redistribute wealth through the United Nations. However, despite the messianic hoopla, the Maitreya refused to appear, a fact predictably blamed on humanity's invocative weakness. As recently as early 1987, Creme's organization, the Tara Center, placed a full-page ad in *U.S.A. Today* proclaiming "The Christ Is in the World."

Another New Age activist, former UN Assistant Secretary-General Robert Muller, is a popular advocate of global spirituality. In a "cosmic age," when earth becomes the "planet of God," humankind will universally seek "no less than its reunion with the divine, its transcendence into ever higher forms of life." So says Muller (1982, 49). It is the UN, he believes, that will play a crucial role in transforming the globe.

Transcendental Meditation continues to be active politically, as well. Under Maharishi Mahesh Yogi, TM plans to bring in the ideal civilization on earth through the "Maharishi unified field." More and more as we tap into the cosmic source of infinite potential (by meditating), all problems will become solvable. The Maharishi unified field is actually the Hindu Brahman (impersonal "all" or "one"), garbed in scientifically respectable Western terms.

Thus, New Age politics ranges from the eccentric and weird to the plausible, from Creme's occult idealism to Satin's skillful pragmatism, exemplified in his political newsletter, *New Options*. But although it may seem a strange conglomeration of forces, the New Age has brought together a growing number of theorists and activists who are stumping for the One. They may be promoting world order, ecology, pagan feminism, disarmament, or meditation in public schools, but they are becoming a force to be recognized.

How can such an eclectic group make a difference? Can it really wield effective political clout?

Granted, New Age political unity is more ideological than organizational. Ferguson says that New Age politics is empowered by New Age assumptions, and these assumptions are bolstered by a web of informational networks. Eventually they will generate power enough to remake society, she says.

In the networking, there is power. Thus, groups and individuals are linked through "conferences, phone calls, air travel, books, phantom organizations, papers, pamphleteering, photocopying, lectures, workshops, parties, grapevines, mutual friends, summit meetings, coalitions, tapes, and newsletters" (Ferguson 1980, 62). New Agers, from health-food-store operators to members of political-action committees, join together to spread their ideas. When Ferguson defines the New Age movement as "a network of networks aimed at social transformation," there is no mistaking the intentions of this movement (Ferguson 1980, 63).

Is it being successful?

At present, that is difficult to gauge. Many who agree with the New Age platform on global unity, ecological concerns, feminism, and other issues, may not be pantheistic. But the New Age movement has a way of capturing an issue.

New Age ideas are finding their way into civil government, and tax dollars are being spent to support them. For example, the Congressional Clearinghouse on the Future, a federal legislative service organized in 1976 to help Congress assess major trends, keeps politicians abreast of the latest research in futurism. It regularly sponsors lectures and dialogues with New Age activists like Capra, Ferguson, Rifkin, and Naisbitt, and its newsletters keep readers well aware of the thinking of these New Age leaders. Thus, the clearinghouse serves as a governmentally sponsored New Age forum, although non-New Age views are also presented.

Politicians of Transformation

Politicians and political parties are catching "transformationalism" as if it were contagious. *Leading Edge*, a now-defunct New Age triweekly on social transformation, carried the headline " 'Transformation' Planks Become Part of Democratic Platform" (1982). Members of the Association for Humanistic Psychology and the New World Alliance have drafted amendments for Democratic Party platforms in the state of California.

In fact, the 1982 Democratic platform even included much of the wording of the transformational platform, endorsing—among other things—"crime prevention through holistic lifestyle changes." The text's conclusion agrees with any New Ager: "Ultimately, all humanity must recognize the essential interconnectedness and interdependence of all human beings and all of nature—humanity has no other choice if we are to stop world annihilation" (*Leading Edge* 1982).

A futurist and prominent New Age spokeswoman, Barbara Marx Hubbard, waged a campaign for the 1984 Democratic vice-presidential nomination, but a New Age newsletter, *Renewal*, lamented that "the transformational synthesis has yet to guide the voting behavior of a U.S. Senator or Representative" (1982).

Overseas, however, New Age politics has been more effective. According to *Renewal*, Sweden is the first country where "transformation-oriented politics has entered the political mainstream," (1980). Sweden sponsored a conference (Living Companies in the New Age), which drew five hundred people, mostly executives, to hear New Age thinkers. The government-run Secretariat for Future Studies serves as an ongoing catalyst.

In Germany, the Green party embodies many New Age viewpoints. The Green perspective is global and seeks to solve the world's crises by stressing the interconnectedness of life. Manon Maren-Grisenbach, who served for two years on the Green's national executive committee, explains its ecological vision: "The emphasis on relations and interconnections . . . is the foundation of Green thought and being" (Capra, Spretnak 1984, 77).

The party's ecological orientation springs from a pantheistic and monistic sentiment that is not strange to German intellectual life. In their favorable book, *Green Politics*, Fritjof Capra and Charlene Spretnak comment that an expression of the Green spirituality is their emphasis on the oneness of humanity and nature, a spirituality "parallel to the principles of Native American, pre-Christian European (that is, Pagan) Taoist, and Buddhist traditions" (Capra and Spretnak, 1984, 54).

Some Greens have also emphasized unilateral disarmament, and, according to *Newsweek* (June 6, 1983), they have received funds from the Soviet Union—who have a vested interest in U.S. disarmament—to this end.

Although the German Greens are struggling to unite competing factions, they are inspiring worldwide emulation. Some New Age activists in the West champion a distinctively "green" political position.

New Agers have other ways of introducing their ideas, in addition to politics. In the United States, New Agers have cooperated effectively with the military. Ferguson notes that the Department of Defense has funded "research projects on meditation, biofeedback, psychic phenomena and alternative medical approaches." Such funding, she thinks, will legitimize ideas "that might otherwise appear 'far out' " (Ferguson 1980, 236).

One such group was the First Earth Battalion, the brainchild of a not-so-traditional United States military think tank called the Delta Force. The battalion, also called The Natural Guard, was projected to be a New Age militia of warrior monks attuned to resolving conflict through Yoga, meditation, and the martial arts.

Power through consciousness is the key. Innovator Jim Channon's operations manual, *Evolutionary Tactics* (1982) says that "God is within each of us" and that the warrior-monk should develop "psiwork," to read minds, travel out of the body, engage in psychokinesis, and even pass through objects. The army paid Channon to produce a multimedia presentation about the battalion for the United States Military Academy's senior class. Channon claims that his concepts have infected the highest ranks of the military. Although the Delta Force is now out of commission, it did inject New Age ideas into the military (Dietrich 1987).

And Channon isn't alone. A recent book called *Mind Wars*, by investigative reporter Ron McRae (1984), reports that research into the military potential of psychic weapons is undeniable and influential.

New Age Moves Into Education

New Age ideas and practices are also infiltrating state-sponsored education. In California, "confluent education" integrated Eastern meditation and pantheistic theology in its curriculum. For some time, Transcendental Meditation introduced its ideas into public education as the Science of Creative Intelligence, until a court ruling declared it religious, and said it violated separation of Church and state.

Nevertheless, some physical-education departments in state universities teach Yoga. For instance, in 1984, a northwestern university offered beginning, intermediate, and advanced classes in *Kundalini* Yoga, which teaches the kindling of *Kundalini* (or "serpent power") at the base of the spine, so the *Kundalini* may travel up various energy centers to the "third eye." Such initiation into the One is sponsored by the state.

Satin's New Age Political Platform advocates the repeal of all compulsory-education laws and supports the use of "humanistic and transpersonal methods . . . that can develop our higher selves, as well as our intellects" (Satin 1978, 250). He also encourages Yoga and other Eastern physical cultures for physical training. Unless Satin wants to dismantle state-sponsored education entirely—which is unlikely—we may assume that he and others will use politics to bring New Age techniques into public schools.

Although society may be hostile to the new consciousness culture, Keys muses that the New Age is an elusive enemy because it is so decentralized. He also says that its emphasis on "the good old pioneering American virtues of self-reliance, thrift, self-discipline and good neighborliness . . . will nullify in advance charges of deviation from desirable norms" (Keys 1982, 88). Linking pantheism with self-reliance ("God is within; we can do it!"), the New Agers are trying to color the political future of America.

What Is the Christian Response?

Though Christians may like some of the New Age proposals (appropriate technology, ecology, and so forth), the difference between Christ and the One is immense. New Age hopes are grounded entirely in human potential, the divine within, and the One for all. Once this psychic beast is unleashed, New Agers say, the world will change. The new mind will make a new world—as soon as the old mind is overthrown.

But as one astute reviewer of Capra's *The Turning Point* put it: "Human ingenuity in creating untold misery did not wait for the development of a mechanistic worldview. . . . The holistic worldviews that have for thousands of years dominated thought in the Far East have not avoided hunger, violence, overpopulation, nor the cultural revolution" (Jahoda 1982, 498).

The Christian believes that political realism must begin with the realization that man is a sinner; New Agers hope in human potential, which is viewed as good and trustworthy. The New Age equates sin with ignorance, believing we can rid ourselves of such ignorance when we accept the enlightenment of pantheism.

The Christian sees such enlightenment as a deceptive counterfeit. The only way that either personal or political consciousness can be raised is by first seeing the reality of sin and the need of redemption through Jesus Christ. All detours around the cross of Christ crash on the brutal rocks of reality. The Christian who hungers and thirsts for political justice looks to God as Lord, Law-Giver, and Judge, not to a godhead within. Christians serve the Savior, not the self. They consult the Scriptures for political instruction.

The Insufficiency of New Age Ethics

When Satin speaks of the dissipation of good and evil into one, you have to wonder what happens to ethics. That is, indeed, a major problem (Satin 1978, 97).

Ferguson is afflicted with similar ambiguity. On the one hand, she claims that with an "awareness of multitude realities, we lose our dogmatic attachment to a single point of view." Yet, on the other hand, she calls for "right power" which you can presume is opposed to "wrong power" (Ferguson 1980, 192).

You can see this same ambiguity in W. I. Thompson's *From Nation to Emanation*. In his sophisticated scheme of things, he tries to transcend all ideologies by uniting opposites. Good does not oppose evil, but interacts with it, cosmically and politically. "No idealogy can express truth. . . . Truth is that which overlights [sic] the conflict of opposed ideologies" (Thompson, 1982, 84). One wonders how Thompson could even know this, since even his own ideology couldn't express truth. Although we can't deny that Thompson's system is elaborately constructed, yet we have to wonder if his judgments have any sure point of reference. In the end, he can appeal only to the planet itself. He concludes that "our planet is a crystalline image of everything we need to know to endure and prevail" (Thompson 1982, 84).

The Christian looks to the creation to see God's glory, but not for ethics, because the world is fallen. For ethical values, we must look beyond the creation, to the Creator and to unchanging biblical values that bear on political life, such as the sanctity of life, the rejection of statism, and the avoidance of the occult.

The Intrigue of the Occult

Beyond these ambiguities and contradictions, New Age politics is riddled with an occult elitism. World Goodwill, for instance, incorporates Bailey's notion of a hierarchy of spiritual beings who will be externalized on earth's spiritual plane, to put the "plan" into effect. David Spangler, board member of Planetary Initiative and much influenced by Bailey, speaks of Lucifer as the angel of man's inner evolution, who will work with the "Christ" to advance humanity's cosmic consciousness. Spangler calls us to a "Luciferic initiation into the New Age." Spangler's *Revelation: The Birth of a New Age* is based on communications received from various spiritual entities. (Spangler 1977, 36, 39).

Both Bailey and Spangler draw from Theosophy, a religion

that esteems Lucifer as an advanced spiritual entity. For Spangler, Lucifer is a great and mighty planetary consciousness, not Satan. Of course, a person who flatters the father of lies (see John 8:44) would not view him as evil. We should remember the apostle Paul's warning that Satan himself masquerades as an angel of light (see 2 Corinthians 11:14).

Just as New Age politics looks to human potential, it also looks to supposedly advanced spiritual entities—even to Lucifer himself. Much New Age inspiration comes from a new type of spiritism. Thompson and Spangler agree that the new order must be hierarchical. All are not fit to lead the planet into the New Age. Until the time when all will realize their divinity and attune themselves to the whole, "it is obvious that in conducting the affairs of a spiritual society one would not turn to those less attuned"(Spangler 1980, 106).

Despite their ostensible objection to totalitarianism and tyranny, New Agers ultimately condone it. Only the cosmically conscious are fit to rule.

These enlightened rulers will transcend any moral law. United with the One through cosmic consciousness, they embody truth. There is no good or evil; the One is beyond such moral distinctions, and the word of the One is final.

One-World Idolatry

For New Agers, a politically unified world has become the reason for a crusade. The age of independence is over; nations must be united and globally guided.

Doug Bandow notes that the policies of the United Nations will place it at the helm: "The UN is drifting away from the goal of establishing an international peaceful order in which economic, as well as political rights, are secure, and is working instead to build a New International Economic Order in which the UN manages global resources" (Bandow 1984, 29).

While many New Agers proclaim the need to maintain unity in diversity for a new world order, for several reasons, pantheism and globalism oppose this type of order. First, a global government needs coercive control and power to govern. It must enforce its rule, economically or militarily. Such intervention would override the national self-determination or autonomy promised in the New Age agenda.

For instance, Muller (1982, 26) says that the United Nations should "never be bypassed by any nation or group of nations as humanity's peacekeeping force." He recommends that it become the planet's central statistical office and data bank and be strengthened regionally, bringing each continent to bear its full contribution and role in the total world order. Such a peacekeeping force would have to be coercive. Big Brother stands at the door and knocks.

As Reinhold Niebuhr pointed out years ago, it is unrealistic to think that superpowers like the Soviet Union will drop their goal of world conquest for a one-world government. "They may use such an idea for their own aggrandizement, but not for their subjugation" (Niebuhr 1953, 18f).

Second, because the New Age says deity resides in humanity, it must unify the new godhead.

As R. J. Rushdoony says, "A divided or disunified god is useless. . . . The deity, in order to exercise the control which is required of him, and in order to be an assured source of certainty, must be united. . . . Accordingly, for the religion of humanity, as represented in the United Nations, the unity of mankind . . . is a necessity" (Rushdoony 1978, 186).

The United Nations, or any other group with global aspirations, must acquire power to unite nations. In the New Agers' agenda, it must lay the brick of a new Babel, proclaiming an order whose ultimate unity and direction opposes the Creator (see Genesis 11:1-9). The ancient world-order enthusiasts in Genesis tried to force the "apostate thesis of ultimate oneness and equality onto all mankind" in order to build a "one-world order and usher in paradise apart from God" (Rushdoony 1979). That is what the New Agers are trying to do today, and their attempt is equally in vain. All towers of Babel are built in vain, apart from the cornerstone of Jesus Christ.

No political institution should claim total power. Since man is imperfect and sinful, political power must be distributed among various institutions and nations. Centralization of power is even more dangerous than the current national diversity.

An idolatrous internationalism must be rejected by Christians. Christ is Lord; neither the nation nor the planet are sovereign. Global government, or what could be termed "the cosmic state," must be rejected as idolatry, since cosmic humanism enthrones man in the place of God.

The horror of such an order is graphically portrayed in Revelation 13, where a cosmic state has usurped all individual and national rights, and where no one can buy or sell without the mark of the beast, which certifies total control. Despite some of the good intentions of New Age world-order advocates, their position lays a blueprint for totalitarianism and tyranny. G. K. Chesterton (1955, 246) once wrote, "Exactly in proportion as you turn monotheism into monism you turn it into despotism."

Jesus Christ came not to unite at all costs, but to divide truth from falsehood, good from evil, and light from darkness (*see* Luke 12:49–53). Unity is a goal that can be attained only by biblical standards. It is not reached by aspiring to a counterfeit Oneness that denies biblical truth.

Satan (Lucifer) offered Christ the kingdoms of the world, if He would worship him. But Christ vetoed Satan's political agenda. "Away from me, Satan! For it is written: 'Worship the Lord your God, and serve him only' " (Matthew 4:10).

Similarly, the New Age offers us the kingdoms of this world, if we worship the god in us. But just as Christ did not accept power on Satan's terms, neither should we. After all, Satan himself first tempted us by saying we would be gods if we usurped the authority of God (*see* Genesis 3:5, 6). We should review the consequences of that first sin and evaluate the New Age appeal accordingly.

And we should also remember that while the summons to "disciple all nations" includes all life and every nation, it excludes any illicit synthesis of truth and falsehood.

Against the One for All

As long as the One gains cultural ground, it will seek to annex political territory. To do this, the New Age must speak in a politically acceptable language, and it must use and infiltrate existing political systems. Knowing this, the Christian must avoid any illicit political compromises and forge a consistent Christian critique and counterproposal.

The world desperately thirsts for new life and ideological vigor, but the transfusion of the One into its veins will only reanimate the old humanistic hulk that beats its rugged and worn fists against the city of God. New policies can never hide the old lie that says humanity yields only to itself, for self is God, and we control our own destiny.

But Christ remains "ruler of the kings of the earth" (Revelation 1:5), and God warns all political impostors: "Therefore, you kings, be wise; be warned, you rulers of the earth. Serve the Lord with fear and rejoice with trembling. Kiss the Son, lest he be angry and you be destroyed in your way, for his wrath can flare up in a moment. Blessed are all who take refuge in him" (Psalms 2:10–12).

6

TRANSPERSONAL PSYCHOLOGY: PSYCHOLOGY AND SALVATION MEET

Frances S. Adeney

THE NEW AGE MOVEMENT FOUND A FRIEND IN TRANSPERSONAL PSYCHOLOGY. Transpersonal psychology is a relatively new field. It depends on a monistic worldview that sees individuals as part of the ultimate fabric of the universe, part of a "divine oneness." It also stresses the worth of persons, their freedom to choose, and their power to "change one's reality"—concepts that flourish in humanistic psychology.

The time seemed right for a branch of psychology that included the spiritual dimension in its thinking.

For years many American psychologists, following the pattern of Freud, had been trying to understand humans without reference to their spiritual dimension. By rejecting the supernatural, psychology had more in common with physiology, sexology, and evolutionary theory than with philosophy and religion. Thus, psychology was cast in a scientific mold.

Behaviorism took science even more seriously. Before long, it became clear that the model of the human used in radical behaviorism left the individual without choice, without responsibility, and without capacity for the nobler traits traditionally connected with the Western view of humanity.

Seeing the problem, a group of humanistic psychologists broke with both behaviorism and psychoanalysis. Reaffirming the dignity and freedom of the human being, these thinkers taught that humankind could reach great potential through self-understanding and individual action. Once again, religious longings were discussed, although the spiritual dimension of life was concerned solely with personal development and self-actualization.

Nevertheless, this third force in psychology opened the door for the entrance of a fuller, more defined spirituality. As humanistic psychology merged with certain religious understandings of life, it became all-encompassing. The spiritual journey became the focus of psychological growth. Soon a spiritualized psychology was trying to explain the meaning of the divine, postulating a view of reality as illusion. Transpersonal psychology was born.

Transpersonal psychology brought ideas of the "divine within" and the oneness of reality (monism) into psychology. Jungian psychology also revived, offering its explanation of the spiritual yearning of humanity, which had been left unexplained by humanistic psychology.

In transpersonal psychology the spiritual journey defines psychological growth. In essence, transpersonal psychology embraces a Westernized pantheism, a view of God that has its roots in Hinduism and Buddhism.

In 1968, when humanistic psychology was still in its adolescence, Abraham Maslow wrote, "I should say also, that I consider Humanistic, Third Force Psychology, to be transitional, a preparation for a still 'higher' Fourth Psychology, transpersonal, transhuman, centered in the cosmos rather than in human needs and interest, going beyond humanness, identity, self-actualization and the like" (iii–iv). Today, what was once the dream of a few idealists has become a fourth force in psychology.

Strictly speaking, transpersonal psychology is not psychology at all. It is a blending of psychological concepts, evolutionary theory, and religious belief; it attempts to give a cosmic explanation for all of life. Transpersonal psychology discusses not the human in the cosmos, but the human *and* the cosmos. In his article, "The Meaning of Everything," transpersonal therapist Arthur Deikman writes more of philosophy and Zen Buddhism than he does of psychology. He defines the individual as "the means whereby reality articulates itself." "I see psychotherapy," he said, "as a spiritual discipline" (Deikman 1972).

Seeking Power in Psychology

Humanistic psychology did, indeed, open the door for religious discussion in psychology, but its approach was human centered. At the apex of its search for meaning was the human being. The self-aware human, living at the height of his or her physical and mental capacity, became the goal of adjustment. Humans were given "science's" permission to worship themselves. Though this philosophy resulted in numerous therapies and self-help groups, it did not fill the religious vacuum felt in our society.

As outlined by humanistic psychologist Abraham Maslow, "being-values" tell us what we ought to be like. Standards of humanity are set high; the giving, open, mature person is held up as an example for us to pattern ourselves after.

Humanistic psychology believes we have the freedom to choose the self-actualized life. We are told that we have infinite potential and that it is within our power to reach high levels of awareness and creativity. Humanistic psychology offers all we ever wanted. Its promises of freedom and choice, control and fulfillment tug us toward hope. We don't want to give up the dream of wholeness that the human-potential movement offers us.

In a similar way, Old Testament law set high standards that humans were expected to meet. The problem is, neither Old Testament law nor twentieth-century humanistic psychology could deliver the power to actualize those dreams of perfection.

We can pretend, to ourselves and others, that the goal has been reached, but sooner or later, we must find a source of power that will really make the goal realizable.

Without a spiritual dimension, humanistic psychology was only a tenuous, fragile philosophy. Consequently, it was inevitable that religious ideas eventually began to infiltrate it, giving people a deepened sense of hope that they could, indeed, become self-actualized.

Did humanistic psychology turn to Christianity for that needed source of power? No; Christianity had been rejected at the outset. Therapists explored other sources of power. The "wisdom within" became a generally accepted alternative to the power Christians found through Christ. Some therapists sought an occult source of wisdom, searching for a spirit guide, discovering psychic powers, and witnessing paranormal events. Others suggested a pantheistic source of wisdom, seeing the divinity of all things. If the physical world is a manifestation of divinity, then each part of it contains that divinity—that wisdom which, unveiled, illuminates the mind and empowers action. Others looked for wisdom from "masters" who, having reached enlightenment, could now guide others.

In this way, Eastern ideas of reality and God entered the realm of psychology. The human-potential movement embraced pantheistic and occult sources of power. The idea of transcending the self, seeking enlightenment through oneness with the universe, blended with the highest goals of humanistic psychology.

All these religious ideas of universal wisdom allow us to continue to center on ourselves. Universal wisdom empowers us from within, via the "inner wisdom," a "higher self," or the "divine within." Nothing is needed from outside; we are self-sufficient. Concepts like these provided hope for individuals who faltered in their struggle for self-actualization.

Thus humanistic psychology found a source of power and was able to accept a religious dimension without denying itself. Any outside source of wisdom was unnecessary; the self continued to reign supreme.

Merging the Transpersonal With the Humanistic

Today many Western therapies show Eastern influences, and Eastern gurus are adopting Western therapies. "Spirit guidance" enters the classroom, and past-life reincarnations inform certain psychotherapies. Transpersonal psychology finds these mergers not only compatible, but enhancing to its ideology. George Leonard, along with others in the human-potential movement, believes that "all around us we can witness a vital, vibrant rebirth taking place" (AHP *Newsletter* 1975).

Esalen is an example. In searching for a spiritual dimension, Esalen turned to monistic and occult traditions (Klein 1979, 20–33). Esalen had begun as a prestigious center for exchange of ideas on human potential: encounter, gestalt, bioenergetics, Zen, and others. By the late 1970s, however, the tone at Esalen had become more spiritual. Jenny O'Connor, a prominent figure at the institute, claimed to be in touch with the highest intelligences in the universe. Those intelligences were called "the Nine," nine spirit guides who directed O'Connor and offered her wisdom and spiritual insight. Currently Esalen embraces much Eastern thought, as well as the occult thinking expressed by O'Connor.

Arica, a philosophy that originated in the East, moved West to merge with humanistic psychology. Founder Oscar Ichazo studied Zen, shamanism, Buddhism, Confucianism, and the I Ching. Coming from that background, he then began teaching at the Institute for Applied Psychology in Chile. In establishing Arica, Ichazo ingeniously combined Christian terminology,

Eastern religious ideas, and Western psychological techniques (mainly gestalt and encounter).

Rajneesh is another thinker who has made the East/West synthesis. No longer a traditional Eastern guru, Rajneesh includes psychotherapeutic techniques in his philosophy. Ram Dass, a Western psychologist, has become an Eastern guru.

Transpersonal thinking in the human-potential movement surfaces also in *est* and its derivatives: Lifespring, Actualizations, and a host of other weekend seminars. Former salesman Werner Erhard put together an intriguing package of Freudian theory, behavior-modification techniques, Eastern philosophy, and humanistic psychology. Rather than explaining away guilt, *est* uses our guilt and sense of failure to get us to give up our old beliefs. People taking *est* training are subjected to an intense barrage of psychological techniques, coupled with sensory deprivation, in an extremely authoritarian context. The program is geared to stripping us of values, mores, and religious beliefs so that we may begin "freely" choosing values and creating our own reality.

Humanistic assumptions of the perfection of the individual and the potential for transcendence are crucial to *est*. As we let go of personal beliefs, *est* philosophy is placed in the gap. The world is illusion; we see whatever we choose to see. We may create anything we like around us and, in fact, all we see is our own creation. Everything, in essence, is one. We are perfect. We are God.

Clearly the human-potential movement is neither staying within the bounds of therapy, nor moving to the confines of the ashram. Transpersonal psychology, although somewhat outside the halls of academia, is growing more influential every year. John F. Kennedy University, in Orinda, California, offers a graduate program in the study of human consciousness that confers M.A. degrees in Interdisciplinary Consciousness Studies, Arts and Consciousness, Transpersonal Counseling Psychology, and Clinical Holistic Health Education, plus an M.S. degree in Parapsychology.

The president of the International Transpersonal Association declared, "It seems to be the perfect time and place to celebrate the increasing convergence of Western physics and Eastern metaphysics, of modern consciousness research and Eastern spiritual systems" (Grof 1981).

Although transpersonal psychology is interpreted in many ways, it can basically be defined as the study of humans with the context of a religious worldview that teaches the essential oneness of all things and the primacy of consciousness in the universe.

With that broad definition in mind, let us examine the basic beliefs of transpersonal psychology.

Consciousness-Is-God

In transpersonal psychology, the ground of all being is consciousness. Consciousness expresses itself in physical reality; it is the tie that binds everything together. Any boundaries we see are illusory. Our perception of things as separate often brings suffering to ourselves and others, because we fail to perceive our oneness with everything.

We can experience the reality of the transpersonal only when those barriers of separateness are broken down. Humankind is evolving, transpersonal psychologists say. We are evolving, they say, from merely physical expressions of consciousness to the pure expression of consciousness that is spirit. We are moving toward "higher consciousness," which can be induced by meditation or "peak experiences." Eventually, they say, evolution will culminate in pure spirit, and consciousness will have returned to its original state.

Of course, such a view is not new. Both Hinduism and Buddhism have propounded an all-encompassing unity, along with the unreality of the physical. By taking this monistic view and Westernizing it, transpersonal psychology has given it the sanction of science.

Huston Smith, professor of religion emeritus at Syracuse University, speaks of humankind mirroring the universe (Smith 1979). The universe, comprising the infinite, God, the psychic, and matter, in that descending order, is mirrored in each person's spirit, soul, mind, and body. (*See* Chart 1.)

Smith supports the idea with examples from the world's great religions. He thinks that a universal way of viewing God and the cosmos was overthrown in modern times, more for methodological reasons rather than for reasons of truth. The empirical model yielded a certain kind of control over nature and a method for knowing that had not been previously available. Now, however, Smith believes that such a model is too limiting. Its usefulness has ended. Everything changed with Einstein's theory, Smith suggests, and a return to a unified view of matter and consciousness is now taking place.

Smith's analysis of human history, religion, and science is intriguing, but a bit too neat. His assertion that all cultures—at all times prior to Western science—shared a single view of truth, is a grave overgeneralization. The Old Testament, for example, depicts many worldview conflicts between Judaism and the beliefs of surrounding cultures. The fact that Western scientific views of reality appeared in the West, rather than the East, indicates a different set of assumptions about the world, which in turn gave rise to a new way of dealing with matter. Pitting the scientific method against all of human tradition greatly oversimplifies the complex questions of reality and truth.

Psychology, too, found the natural-science model too limiting for a thorough discussion of the nature of humankind. A return to a monistic understanding of reality is, however, only one option. Smith argues that it is the sole option.

The conclusion that consciousness is all-pervading presents a particular view of God. God is no longer *other*—out there, separate from humanity—and perhaps communicating to humans through the Holy Spirit, Jesus, or a written revelation. In Smith's view of God, consciousness was and is and will be. As we touch this consciousness, we become enlightened. We realize our own godlikeness, our participation in the divinity of all things. Such a view of God is a basic component of transpersonal psychology.

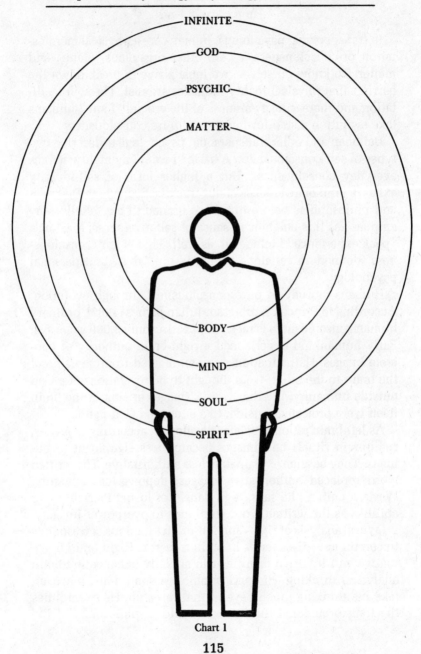

Chart 1

Humanity Is God

In transpersonal psychology, humans are a physical manifestation of consciousness, as are other organisms, plants, and matter. To know ourselves, we must strive to break down the barriers that physical reality indicates are real. Through meditation and increasing awareness of the crucial "I am," humans take evolution a step further toward pure consciousness.

Deikman and other transpersonal psychologists describe two types of self-consciousness. A basic "I want" mentality defines everyday consciousness. But a higher form of self-identity exists, a kind of awareness of our true essence, which Deikman and philosophers before him have termed "I am." Rollo May emphasizes this heightened sense of self-awareness; Maslow's "peak experience" includes it, as well. This "I am" consciousness, defined in religious terms, is crucial to transpersonal psychology.

Humans journey to pure consciousness through evolution. According to Princeton professor Julian Jaynes (1982), ordinary human consciousness is recent, appearing only 3,000 years ago. Early humankind experienced a right-brain authority of concrete images. Hallucinations, communicated from one side of the brain to the other, were thought to be revelations of a God outside humanity. In other words, images arising in the brain itself were projected outside, to a supposed God figure.

As left-brain rationality later developed, according to Jaynes, right-brain rituals and images became less significant to humans. They became explainable, less authoritative. The written word replaced authoritative images, depowering humanity. Western culture, he says, is in danger of losing its right-brain abilities as the written word continues to overpower imagery.

Jaynes' analysis of right- and left-brain functions corresponds to certain new discoveries in brain research. Right-brain imaginative and intuitive faculties can actually enhance left-brain analytical thinking. His philosophical assumptions, however, take his thinking much beyond that research. He exemplifies the transformational thinker who builds a philosophy of life and a hope for the future on a thin base of scientific research. According to Jaynes, fully utilizing and integrating both left- and right-brain faculties will bring humanity to a higher evolutionary plateau (Jaynes 1982). Further, humankind has a purpose: to evolve, and thus to return to pure consciousness, or God. Individual lives then have meaning in elevating the course of evolution. We can take hold of our destiny, the transpersonal thinkers affirm, not in a behavioristic or humanistic sense, but in a cosmic/religious sense. We, as individuals, can cause the culmination of history to come closer by increasingly striving to reach that higher consciousness.

Transcendental Meditation, Maharishi Mahesh Yogi's system of meditation for the Westerner, illustrates this same principle. TM teaches that as more persons meditate and get in touch with consciousness, the world becomes a better place; it becomes more spiritual and less physical. Therefore, wars and fighting will lessen as more people meditate. Consciousness combats evil as differences are seen to be illusions. The world itself, TM claims, thus evolves to a more divine state.

Est's Hunger Project describes the practical results of this process. If all individuals create their own reality, we can change reality by changing our perceptions of it. As we think or meditate on fullness rather than hunger, on satisfaction rather than need, reality becomes more full and hunger is lessened. The Hunger Project believes that hunger will end—literally—in higher consciousness.

The World Is God

This brings us to the view of the world held in transpersonal psychology. Again, consciousness is at its base. Transpersonal psychology holds that the world itself is our perception of it. As we experience the world differently, so it becomes different. As we realize the oneness of all reality, we become one with the divine. The hope is that one day humans will evolve to the point where this physical reality—this world of suffering—will disintegrate and pure spirit will again prevail.

Clearly, transpersonal psychology has shifted to a religious orientation in its concerns. Its focus is not on either our inner struggles or our external behavior. Transpersonal psychology discusses humanity as part of the cosmos, connected to and evolving toward pure spirit, the true expression of consciousness.

A New Synthesis

Transpersonal thinking is a new synthesis in twentieth-century thought. Today transpersonal ideas are discussed not only in psychology, but also in education, history, evolutionary theory, physics, and brain theory. In psychology, Maslow's "peak experience" flows directly into higher levels of consciousness. In education, teaching techniques that emphasize feelings merge with the idea that all wisdom lies within the child: The universal mind in each one is simply waiting to be awakened. Evolutionary thinking, linked with pantheistic concepts of universal unity, forms a religious/scientific view of evolution, a totally new concept in evolutionary theory.

Evolution towards consciousness is the key concept in this synthesis. It is in evolution that the religious and the scientific meet. Transpersonal thinking modifies Darwinian evolutionary theory by adding a religious dimension to it—a dimension of purpose. Humans are no longer worshiping the self per se, but are worshiping universal consciousness as found through the self. Thus, religious ideals return to academic analysis.

Now transpersonal psychology is taking its beliefs to the American public. For example, John Naisbitt writes, in the best-seller *Megatrends* (1982), "By discovering our potential as human beings, we participate in the evolution of the human race. We develop the inner knowledge, the wisdom, perhaps, required to guide our exploration."

In its emphasis on evolutionary development, transpersonal psychology traces its heritage to nineteenth-century European thought. Freud taught that evolutionary history was embodied in each individual. He taught that people live through stages of earlier human development as part of their individual psychological growth. That concept is now more fully developed in transpersonal psychology's stages of evolutionary development toward consciousness.

Carl Jung also contributed to transpersonal psychology. Jung firmly believed in a super-rational mode of knowing. His earliest dreams, and many later instances of personal intuition, contained knowledge he believed he could not humanly have possessed. He attributed this knowledge to a collective unconscious that was common to all (Jung 1961). Through the collective unconscious, we are linked to cultures of the past, as well as to all humankind, he believed. The memory of the species, so to speak, is contained in the collective unconscious, and people act out of the collective history embedded in their unconscious.

Jung clung to the spiritual side of human nature. In his earliest years, his connection to the spiritual consisted of a father whose Christian faith Jung pitied rather than respected. His metaphysically inclined mother displayed a powerful personality at times, and young Carl Jung was frightened by her activities. His early dreams and later séance experiences confirmed to him the reality of something other than the physical, time-bound world that Freud saw.

Jung outlined four modes of knowing:

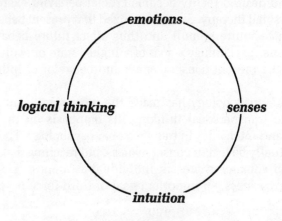

119

For Jung, intuition was the human connection with the spiritual world. Through intuition, he believed, we can get in touch with the collective unconscious—the source of knowledge that leads to a higher knowing.

Jung's collective unconscious parallels transpersonal psychology's concept of the wisdom of the universe contained within the individual. Jung's theory also postulates a dark and light side of the personality, plus masculine and feminine components that must be recognized and synthesized. Apparent contradictions are resolved in a higher unity. Collective archetypes clash within a person, becoming reconciled only on a higher plane of consciousness (Raschke 1980, 149).

Carl Rogers said of Jung, "Jung, perhaps more profoundly than either Adler or Rank, turned toward the idea of the development of an ultimately self-determined spiritual being that transcends the biological forces acting on man" (Evans 1975, xxiv).

Contributions to Transpersonal Psychology

Behaviorism contributed to transpersonal psychology indirectly by turning the attention of psychologists toward actions. Both humanistic and transpersonal psychologies emphasize the importance of individual behavior. Perceiving rightly and "imaging" a desired reality become crucial behavior exercises in transpersonal therapy. Skinner realized that present behavior can influence future stimuli and thus affect future behavior. Transpersonal psychology's goal of a higher state of evolution hinges on the present consciousness and behavior of individuals.

Third-force psychology has made the most significant contribution to transpersonal thinking. Its emphasis on the self continues and intensifies in transpersonal psychology. The self must eventually be lost in consciousness, but reaching that goal depends on enhancing present individual awareness. Heightened self-awareness, an important goal of third-force psychology, becomes even more crucial when human evolution and hope for humankind depend on personal awareness.

All of the major beliefs of humanistic psychology are retained *and spiritually explained* by transpersonal psychology. Experience as the measure of reality, emphasis on personal choice and power, centrality of the self, and change as a vital component of life—each of these beliefs is furthered by transpersonal psychology.

The transition between the two has, therefore, been smooth. Anthony Sutich, founder of the Association for Humanistic Psychology, also began the Association for Transpersonal Psychology. Transpersonal topics are freely aired at the AHP annual conventions, which include seminars on phases of the inner journey, archetypal dreams, T'ai Chi and gestalt connections, aikido, the value of ritualization, evolving personal myths, and so on. At the 1975 conference, Jonas Salk spoke on evolution. One listener, Connie Houle, remarked, "It was like having a glimpse into the creative process itself, a process which ultimately, if we use our new human realization that we do have a choice, can transform and save the world" (Houle 1975).

Here indeed is a remarkable synthesis: a monistic worldview merged with third-force psychology, and an evolutionary theory enfleshed in a religious hope that humans, by their own choice, can save the world.

Ken Wilber

Ken Wilber is a leading figure in transpersonal psychology. In his most scholarly work, *The Atman Project,* Wilber traces the stages of psychological growth through fourteen levels. These levels of growth mirror the seven Yogic chakras. At the "most realized" state, he claims, we experience higher consciousness, which has been the goal of mystics throughout the ages, and is the essence of Maslow's "peak experience" as well as the climax of transpersonal psychology. At this stage, we are in touch with the divine; the physical is lost in the spiritual; we become enlightened.

In a later book, *Up From Eden* (1981), Wilber uses those same stages as a pattern of human evolution. Those major stages of evolution are comparable not only to the seven yogic chakras, but also to the Sefiroth of the Kabbalah, the Sheaths of Hinduism, and Maslow's hierarchy of human needs (Ingrasci 1982, 35). Stages of ignorance yield to levels of consciousness that will eventually result in a return to the spiritual. The final culmination of evolution will be entrance into the Void, the loss of individual personality, and the unity of all things.

Wilber asserts that individual growth is a microcosm of human evolution. We may become stuck at any one stage or go on to fulfill all seven stages, thus reaching enlightenment. At each stage of evolution, sages and mystics have been at higher evolutionary stages than those around them. Those persons prefigure higher forms. Each individual passes through lower evolutionary stages into the present human state, and then may progress even higher, to become a prophet or a seer of the age.

Wilber sees evolution as the basis of hope for humankind's future. In his thinking, he brings together strands of Darwinian evolution, behavioristic models of conditioning, humanistic concepts of the centrality of the self, and a religious orientation that explains the goal of evolution.

He claims that modern evolutionary theorists have all left the Darwinian concept of natural selection. In fact, according to Wilber, a higher power must be assumed for evolution to be possible at all. Of course he disagrees with the "special creationists" theory that God made the world without evolutionary influence at all. Neither does he accept time and chance alone as an explanation for the development of the world as we know it. Rather, Wilber returns to the pantheistic view that matter is a manifestation of the divine and is working its way back to pure spirit.

In Wilber's view, Maslow's "peak experience" becomes thoroughly religious. The Buddha, for example, was one who received such enlightenment. But rather than lose himself in the void, he chose to retain his physical body so he might help others on the path to enlightenment.

Here psychology outlines salvation for humankind. Our own personal growth may result in enlightenment. We personally may reach the next stage of evolutionary growth. And perhaps the children of the next generation will be more enlightened than we are.

To Wilber, individual personality acts as a roadblock to this evolution. He states (1981a):

> And mankind will never, but never, give up this type of murderous aggression, war, oppression, and repression, attachment and exploitation, until men and women give up that property called personality. Until, that is, they awaken to the transpersonal. Until that time, guilt, murder, property, and personality will always remain synonymous.

Dangers of Transpersonal Thinking

Since transpersonal psychology seeks to explain the meaning of everything, numerous strands of thought are brought into its theory. Brain research, the new physics, mythology, and the imagination all receive considerable attention. Meditation, awareness exercises, bodywork, dreamwork, and imaging techniques are studied. Psychic phenomena such as precognition, telekinesis, and automatic writing or drawing increase in importance as the physical world is viewed as a mask for the true wholeness of reality.

Einstein's work is seen by transpersonal thinkers as a watershed in our human perception of reality. Fritjof Capra's recent studies in physics are also cited as evidence that the basis of matter may not be as solid as particle theory once declared.

Such discoveries bring real advances in scientific understanding. They are, however, often quoted as evidence for the philosophical and religious view that consciousness is the basis of reality, that the physical world is not stable or perma-

search not for the wisdom within, but for the wisdom from above. To know the transcendent God, the personal, infinite Creator, and to know that Jesus Christ is God, a Christian looks to the revelation of the Bible and to the work of God's Spirit through the Church and in his own heart.

A Christian understanding of reality is not totally subjective. Although persons might experience reality differently, a common reality is still there to be experienced. There is a truth to be known: An objective world exists, although it may be interpreted in various ways. The Christian is not lost in a sea of subjective impressions but is grounded in a real world, in which actions have meaning, moral content, and consequences.

Christian Worldview	Worldview of Transpersonal Psychology
GOD	**GOD**
• Creator/sustainer	• Universal consciousness
• Is separate from, uncontrolled by, humans	• Is present in, and part of, all things
HUMANITY	**HUMANITY**
• Made in the image of God, yet fallen	• Manifestation of consciousness
• Finds fulfillment and power through relationship with God	• Contains all wisdom; mirror image of the whole universe
	• Finds fulfillment and power through evolution toward consciousness
WORLD	**WORLD**
• Reality of material world	• Various realities/illusion of the physical
• Part of a moral universe in which absolutes exist	• Oneness of all things
• Real spiritual forces are operative	• Evolution toward pure spirit; that is, consciousness

Christian Critique

Christianity defines and understands humanity in relation to God and His creation, the world. Well-adjusted, healthy people understand their creatureliness and bow to their Creator. Forgiveness and power to live a fully human life are found through Jesus, our path to God.

The path of transpersonal psychology rules out such understanding. God is effectively silenced when the concept of God is incorporated into humanity itself. When that happens, a God outside of ourselves seems unnecessary.

Transpersonal psychology's view of God as consciousness and its view of the world as a manifestation of consciousness delve into the religious mysteries of life. But Christians have a different understanding of those mysteries.

Summary

Humanistic psychology's attempt to redefine its field in more human terms allowed psychology to rediscover humankind's spiritual dimension. Transpersonal psychology defines that spiritual dimension in pantheistic terms, depicting a world of illusion, a god of higher consciousness, and an evolution of the universe back to spirit. Transpersonal psychology is cross-disciplinary, gathering insights from various fields of study. The overarching theory developed from those insights is *religious*, focusing on a universal consciousness, the power behind all things.

In effect, transpersonal psychology postulates a source of outside power without giving up the centrality of the individual self. Universal wisdom is greater than the self, yet it is contained within the self. Without giving up the worship of the self, this meta-psychology attempts to explain "the meaning of everything." By accepting a "divine within," transpersonal psychology has silenced the question of God, diverting many who need renewal from seeking the true God, who could bring healing to their lives.

PART THREE

WHEAT OR TARES— ASSESSMENT

7

TANTRA: UNRAVELING THE COSMOS

Brooks Alexander

NEW AGE PHILOSOPHY IS A MIXTURE OF MANY ELEMENTS. SOME OF IT comes from Hinduism and other Eastern religions. Some of it comes from more modern and secular sources, specifically the language of science and speculative psychotherapy. As the philosophers would say, New Age philosophy is eclectic and syncretistic.

But there is a coherent worldview beneath all the eclectic ornamentation. C. S. Lewis called that worldview pantheism, and identified it as "the only really formidable opponent" to Christianity.

That underlying worldview takes various forms, in various times and cultures. Basically, it is a deification of nature, a worship of natural processes and energies. It inevitably becomes a deification of life and the life force, a worship of the dynamism of vitality. As the apostle Paul revealed in Romans

1:18–25, it is the fundamental religious error of fallen human beings (a category that includes us all).

In the East, that worldview is pervasive, and often religiously institutionalized. In the West, it has been less influential, partly because of its inherent opposition to the dominant, christianized culture. In the religious history of the West, it chiefly appears as either occultism or gnosticism, depending on how closely it approaches or impinges on orthodox Christianity.

The pantheistic worldview predictably achieved its most thorough development in the East. One could point to many ripe examples of "natural religion" in Asia, and most of them have also been rich sources of inspiration for the New Age movement.

But one Eastern teaching in particular represents a comprehensive and systematic elaboration of that underlying religious deviance common to all mankind. That teaching is called *tantra*.

At first, tantra may seem a rather esoteric subject, but its impact has been considerable, even when not named or recognized. In fact, the influence of what we loosely call Eastern religious traditions in the West has largely been that of tantra. Nearly all of the prominent gurus of Yogic enlightenment who have come West have been tantrics: Vivekananda, Yogananda, Maharishi (TM), Maharaj ji (DLM), Muktananda, Rajneesh, and so forth. Whether we knew it or not, our fascination with Eastern spirituality in general has been a fascination with tantra in particular. It has thus played a significant role in the "mystification" of Western culture.

Tantra is critical to understanding the New Age movement for two reasons: First, because the less-developed forms of pantheism are better understood in light of its more developed forms; second, because tantra itself has contributed directly and heavily to all aspects of the New Age movement and its antecedents.

Tantra's distinguishing feature is its sexual emphasis. Philosophically, that translates into notions of polarity as the basis of existence. In fact, it is precisely the rhetoric of polarity that has been most fully assimilated by New Agers, and most widely disseminated by them.

Consequently, much popular culture and many current attitudes reflect the spirit of tantra, even when not influenced by it directly. Characteristically tantric, for example, are the popular notions that individual and social ills will be cured by balancing the hemispheres of the brain or by exalting the "feminine" in order to offset "masculine" extremes.

As tantra—in concert with other compatible beliefs and practices—becomes more deeply entrenched and widespread in the mainstream culture, consensus thinking will increasingly address the woes of humanity in a typically tantric way.

But what is tantra? It is notably hard to define, and even harder to understand. It has been variously mystified, sensationalized, and debunked.

In its broadest definition, tantra is a transreligious tradition. Tantra began as a resurgence of suppressed fertility worship; it ended by penetrating, even permeating, existing religions.

Modern-day tantra is identified most visibly with Tibetan Buddhism. But tantric teachings and scriptures exist in a variety of religious traditions: Hindu, Buddhist, Sikh, Jain, Taoist, and Islamic. In addition to Tibet, which institutionalized tantra, Kashmir, Bengal, and South India have been among the most active centers of tantric practice and dissemination.

The origins of tantra are hidden from view, due in part to Indian culture's indifference to history and documentation. We do know that tantra appeared suddenly: Around A.D. 600 tantric religion was unknown. By A.D. 900 sixty-four tantric scriptures can be identified by name.

Modern historians tend to see tantra as an eclectic teaching that has its roots far back in India's ancient, pre-Aryan religion—a magical, mystical fertility cult that worshiped the great goddess and the female powers of generation.

The best guess from current evidence is that pre-Aryan fertility themes were combined with dualistic philosophy and other elements in an area somewhere west of India during the early centuries A.D. Tantra was created from that mixture.

Eliade (1969) believes that tantra represents the spiritual counterattack of an indigenous mother-cult that had been suppressed by Aryan conquerors.

In any case, tantrics encountered intense opposition and persecution for their unorthodoxy—first from the Aryan establishment and later from the Moslems. Outside the Aryan domain, tantra encountered less resistance. Tantric teachings spread rapidly through Kashmir, Bengal, and Tibet, reaching China and, eventually, Japan.

Tantra has shown that it can fill many cultural forms. It therefore has many appearances. Sometimes it seems like a high spiritual path, sometimes it looks like black magic. It holds itself up as sober realism, yet often seems like systematic insanity with a thin religious gloss.

Tantra also embodies all the extremes and contradictions that it thrives on. It is simultaneously erotic and ascetic, self-indulgent and self-denying. Its rituals invoke demons and deities indiscriminately, yet its doctrine dismisses them all in the name of radical monism. Tantra's adherents range from the respectable to the scandalous, from the credentialed scholar pursuing Sanskrit etymology to the illiterate yogi practicing unspeakable graveyard rituals in the dead of night.

Because of its sexual rituals and its occult components, tantra has been sensationalized more often than understood. If we approach tantra with the wrong assumptions, it will appear confusing and incoherent, or just willfully vile.

Tantra is baffling to the Western mind because it is a religion of opposites. It cultivates contradiction and paradox. Tantra strives for the fusion of opposites on a massive scale, from the top to the bottom of the universe. Ultimately it seeks to dissolve even the dualities that support existence itself.

We should also understand that to the tantric, all apparent paradoxes, oppositions, and contradictions are dissolved in the experiences of "cosmic unity," a mystical union with the One. Tantra becomes truly coherent only through that experience and the practices used to produce it.

Tantric Philosophy

The view of reality that lies behind tantric experience and practice is very much in harmony with classical Hindu metaphysics as expressed in the *Vedas* and *Upanishads*. Like orthodox vedanta philosophy, tantra asserts that reality is One and that the One is the only real. Like vedanta, it recognizes that the world of mind and senses (i.e., ordinary reality) is a world of *maya*—a flicker of shadows and a veil of illusion. This world of apparent form and substance is realy *lila,* the play of divine consciousness—the illusionary magic of duality.

Tantra's shocking uniqueness is that it does not scorn this realm of *maya* as the source of temptation and bondage, but embraces it as the raw material of enlightenment. Tantra sees the realm of maya as the only available context of liberation because the realm of maya is precisely where the unenlightened mind is trapped. If ignorance and delusion are the prevailing condition, then enlightenment must begin amidst the artifacts of ignorance and the phenomena of delusion.

The tantric accepts lila, the play of consciousness, as an arena for knowing the powers of consciousness, then uses those powers as a vehicle of enlightenment, thereby transcending lila altogether.

To the tantric, the universe is a mystical tissue of consciousness, held in form by the tensions of duality—the polar opposites of positive and negative, light and dark, male and female, yang and yin—that appear throughout all levels of existence. Tantra is a way to master these fundamental cosmic dualities through the mastery of one's sexual function.

The connection between sex and cosmic sorcery is based on the theory of "occult correspondence." Polarity is the key to existence; its tensions give unity and structure to all of manifest reality. The human body, as part of manifest reality, is caught in this network of polarity and existence. The body is a microcosm, a miniature version of the cosmos. Polarity in the body (sex) is therefore the key to our own existence. It is also an antenna, tuned to energies of polarity that span the universe.

By learning to control the energies of polarity in the body (i.e. the sexual function), the tantric taps the powers of matter and mind, and masters the secrets of space and time.

Tantra thus embraces illusion as a means to reality, baptizes duality as a path to the One, and affirms the human body—particularly the sexual function—as our most reliable connection with the divine.

But even in its affirmations, tantra is haunted by paradox. The naturalness of human life is affirmed, but only as a means for its ultimate dissolution. Human existence is validated, but only as a platform for leaving humanity behind.

In order to understand this relationship more fully, we will have to look at tantra's theories of the nature of existence: what it is, and where it comes from.

Cycles of Infinity and the Madness of God

In the place beyond time, there is no beginning, and pure consciousness rests in perfect equilibrium. This consciousness is total, fusing all polarities into an undifferentiated unity—a limitless sea of pure potency, without distinction, form, or manifestation. This consciousness is "god." It is all there is.

But something disturbs this primal equilibrium, and the divine stability turns to an oscillating imbalance. The primal duality appears. Male and female are separated: God is divided. The interaction of these primal qualities of consciousness produces a series of waves that further disturb the tranquil surface of the sea of bliss. As these waves vibrate back and forth and further cross and recross one another, their patterns become more elaborate. They also become more "solid," and by degrees condense into "matter." This process of divine devolution eventually extrudes the cosmos as a series of densified pulses, or waves, of compacted vibration.

The tantric universe, then, consists of divine emanations which have become so convoluted that their divinity is concealed. In biblical terms, the creation equals the Fall. In tantric terms, existence equals metaphysical ignorance by definition. Creation only happens when god's mind becomes unbalanced—not "as it were," but quite literally. In this view, creation simply is the insanity of god, and this is the essential meaning of lila.

At the point of maximum illusion, when consciousness has been deeply "materialized," this process of emanation reverses itself. As consciousness moves toward reunion and liberation, the residue of maya that remains becomes intensified. It is compacted as it approaches dissolution. Thus humanity shares in the downward, delusionary course of maya, as the end of all things approaches.

Epochs of Decadence

Human history, as a result, is the sad account of human degeneration. The downward spiritual course of humanity parallels the descent of Mind into bondage to illusion. This deepening decadence spans four distinct ages, or *yugas*, each shorter and more depraved than the last. From the Golden Age of truth and righteousness (*Sat Yuga*) at the dawn of human existence, we have now spiraled out of control into the depths of the fourth and final age of alienation: the Kali Yuga, a period of ignorance, passion, violence, and spiritual darkness. The Kali Yuga will end in the universal fires of destruction and purification.

Tantra offers itself as the path to enlightenment for the Kali Yuga. Other systems were fine back in the Sat Yuga, when people lived much longer than we do today. For us in the Kali Yuga time is short, and we need rapid solutions based on techniques that are powerful enough to produce immediate results.

The Short Path

Enlightenment has often been compared to a mountaintop. The older spiritual paths are like a gradual ascent—more

137

leisurely, but longer, taking many lifetimes to complete. Tantra offers itself as a shortcut to enlightenment, a trip straight up the side of the mountain: liberation in one lifetime. Thus tantra is often called the short path.

But the shortcut has its price. It is both more dangerous and more demanding. The discipline required is rigorous, and the risks are considerable, including insanity, death, and damnation.

In the Kali Yuga, the veils of maya are thick; the delusions of material existence are heavy and cannot be gracefully juggled. They must be forcibly undone and dismantled from within—abolished, dissolved, destroyed.

To us of the Kali Yuga, thoroughly deluded and unable to see beyond the illusions of maya, the tantric goal will seem to be simply the destruction of the world. Thus it is by a profound logic that Shiva, the Hindu god of death and dissolution, is the sponsoring deity of most tantrism. In obedience to this same logic, tantrism has regularly spawned "outlaw" sects, dedicated to death in an aggressively literal way. Tantric cults such as the *Thugee* (from which we get the word *thug*) and *Pindaris* turned random murder into acts of ritual worship.

Shiva is also the god of ecstasy, of divine madness. He personifies *lila* as the insanity of god. Tantrics worship Shiva, and they accept their existence as the insanity of god with no questions asked. The tantrics' novel response is to get gleefully insane along with god, as god, in the midst of existence, and thereby penetrate beyond existence altogether.

Kundalini: To Wake the Snake

Tantra's most important and unique characteristic is its use of sexual imagery to portray enlightenment, the return to Oneness beyond duality.

One of the most familiar versions of this symbolism is the Kundalini myth associated with Indian tantra in particular. Connected with the Kundalini mythology is an elaborate occult system that sees the human body as a network of channels for divine and cosmic energy. Where these channels cross, they create pulse points of psychic and spiritual energy in the body, known as *chakras*. There are said to be some 88,000 chakras throughout the human body, but

> . . . of these, only seven are considered to be of supreme importance, and these are situated along the central axis of the subtle anatomy that runs from tailbone to skull (Walker 1982, 41–42).

Kundalini is the name of the female half of the divine polarity in humankind, which now lies dormant at the base of the spine, separated from her divine lover and masculine counterpart, Shiva. When Kundalini has been awakened, as a result of secret Yogic techniques, she rises through the chakras of the spine toward reunion with Shiva at the crown of the head. When god and goddess unite in sexual embrace, enlightenment occurs, illusion vanishes, and there is only One.

The Kundalini mythology is supported by a vast pop-occult literature in the West. It may come as a surprise, therefore, to learn that many tantrics, particularly Buddhist tantrics, do not accept the reality of Kundalini itself or pay much attention to the *chakra* system on which it is based.

Tantric Practice

Despite its diversities, tantric doctrine is unified by two things: Its imagery is ultimately sexual, and its purpose is ultimately practical. Tantrism, above all, is what one *does* to produce certain states of consciousness. The tantric doctrines are simply interpretations of those states.

For tantra, the surest way to manipulate the mind is to manipulate the functions of the body. The body/mind is really a single unit, in the tantric view, so techniques applied on one level affect what happens on the other. For that matter, every aspect of nature corresponds to something in the spiritual world, and vice versa. The human body is part of this network of correspondences; each aspect of our anatomy has cosmic significance and can be a source of connection with cosmic powers for those who know the secret techniques of psychophysical attunement.

Tantra's emphasis on the body as an instrument of enlightenment leads naturally to a quest for bodily perfection.

> It is believed that only when the body is perfectly attuned and strengthened can it experience and sustain the full intensity of the cosmic state (Mookerjee and Khanna 1977, 21).

This bodily fascination fosters an elitism that can take peculiar forms. In many tantric sects, a person who suffers from any form of physical defect is considered disqualified for salvation.

Tantrism uses several bodily functions as a basis for techniques of enlightenment. The sexual function is the best known of these, but it is not the only one. The functions of posture, sight, breathing, speech, and hearing also provide important tools for enlightenment.

Mantra: The Sound of Salvation

Mantra is one technique that universally characterizes tantra. Mantras are secret sounds, or words of power. Like other tantric techniques, the use of mantra is based on the concept of occult correspondence: The world is vibration (another form of polarity); sound is one form of vibration. Ultimately, all vibrations resonate together. The specific vibrations of a mantra resonate with specific aspects of spiritual reality. When the forces that are awakened in the mind and body become attuned to the corresponding cosmic forces, then the tantric becomes united, or identified, with the transcendent forces personified as gods and goddesses.

Transcendental Meditation's Maharishi Mahesh Yogi speaks from the heart of the tantric tradition when he describes mantras as "chanting to produce an effect in some other world, draw the attention of those higher beings or gods living there" (Maharishi Mahesh Yogi 1968, 17–18).

There are both audible and subtle mantras. Audible mantras are vocally repeated in tantric meditations; subtle mantras are unvoiced but mentally "heard."

> However done, a mantra is enriched, empowered, and activated by repetition. . . . The repetition helps to induce a zenophrenic or trance-like state and bring on mystical illumination (Walker 1982, 24).

In addition to mantras for the "high magic" of enlightenment, tantrism also has mantras for the "low magic" of manipulation. There are mantras for every purpose, be it base or exalted.

In the last analysis, mantra as a technique of enlightenment perfectly displays the tantric paradox. Mantra is rooted in language, yet it undoes language by severing sense from sound. In fact, mantra repetition as a technique is itself the annihilation of language:

> All indefinite repetition leads to the destruction of language; in some mystical traditions, this destruction appears to be the condition for further experiences (Eliade 1969, 216).

Mantra is what language becomes in the process of coming undone.

Yantra: The Diagram of Divinity

A *yantra* is a visual depiction of the same forces that are represented mythologically by the gods and goddesses and audibly by the mantras. Yet yantras are not pictures of the gods, though such divine portraits also abound in tantrism.

141

Just as a mantra is a sound equivalent, the yantra is
a diagrammatic equivalent of the deity and consists
of linear and spatial geometric permutations of the
deity (Mookerjee and Khanna 1977, 33).

Yantras are generally geometrical figures, abstract symbols,
and obscure, complex designs that are sometimes tinted and
are normally drawn, painted, or engraved on a flat surface.
Sometimes they are rendered in three-dimensional form. Most
of these objects are extremely simple, since they are regarded as
tangible manifestations of very basic cosmic energies. One
example, common in Indian tantra, is the so-called *shiva-
lingam*. It is usually a smooth stone in the shape of an
elongated egg, taken to represent the lingam (phallus) of the
god Shiva. Another such three-dimensional symbol is the
yoni-lingam, which portrays the male and female genitals
united.

The vast majority of yantras are two-dimensional diagrams.
The version of this theme most familiar to Westerners is
probably the elaborate form called *mandala*. The word *mandala* means "circle," and mandalas commonly come in the
shape of a circle enclosing a square. Within the outline of the
mandala is an arrangement of smaller shapes and spaces
creating a series of zones, or levels, which radiate from a central
source, evoking the idea of emanation. All of these spaces are
filled with painted scenes: depictions of deities and demons,
levels of heaven and hell, scenes of world creation and world
destruction, and so forth.

Both the mandala and the yantra act as a cosmogram and a
psychogram—that is, they portray the relationship of the qualities of consciousness within the divine mind and also the
analogous order of relationships in the human mind. In this
network of occult correspondences, mandala and yantra give
access to a multidimensional reality. The image becomes an
interface with the dimensions it depicts. The symbol is a point
of contact with the forces it expresses.

Yoga: The Body as Talisman

In addition to meditations on mantra, yantra, and mandala, many forms of tantrism incorporate Yoga in their arsenal of psychotechnologies.

Yoga, of course, is not original to tantra, nor peculiar to it. The various schools of Yoga in India arose and developed more or less independently of tantra. The tantrics commandeered whatever techniques seemed effective and applied them within their own religious system.

Hatha Yoga in particular was appropriated by tantrism, because hatha is the Yoga of physical culture. Like tantra, hatha concentrates on the human body and its invisible (occult) spiritual properties. It also had several specific bodily objectives that were of great interest to tantrics. Chief among them was

> control over certain autonomic functions . . . such as body temperature, the pulse rate, and the reflexes that cause erection and ejaculation, besides an overall stamina to fit it [the body] for the strains of tantric sexual practices, with the ultimate aim of achieving supernatural powers and making the body perfect and immutable (Walker 1982, 37).

Hatha Yoga techniques that are emphasized in tantrism are *asana* (postures) and *pranayama* (breathing exercises).

Pranayama, the practice of breath control, arises logically from the context of occult correspondences. What is breathing, after all, but a form of vibration: the steady, unceasing alternation of in and out that seems the source of life itself. Indeed, to the tantric, breath is the vibratory form that the life force takes as its human fountainhead. By controlling the vibratory rate of this basic life function, the tantric seeks to manipulate the life force it embodies: "There are specific ratios for curing specific diseases, and for giving strength to the various parts of the body" (Walker 1982, 70).

Asana means "seat easily held," though a less-apt description can hardly be imagined from the standpoint of the novice disciple. Many of the postures that hatha Yoga prescribes are difficult to assume and painful to maintain. The rationale for these unusual positions is that the body is continuously channeling currents of spiritual energy. Yogic postures redirect the flow of those currents in the process of bending, twisting, and aligning the body.

Mudra is another practice that is really a resonance of asana on a finer scale. Mudra refers to gestures that are formed by positioning the hands and fingers in a prescribed way.

All of these techniques, and others, can be practiced independently. Ultimately, however, the goal of tantrism is to attune the body/mind at all levels simultaneously by employing a number of techniques as parts of an elaborately choreographed ritual. Such a set of coordinated practices is called *mahamudra* (great posture) or *paramudra* (supreme posture).

> The *paramudra* ... is a combination of bodily attitude (*asana*), breath control (*pranayama*), hand gesture (*mudra*) ... and meditation on mystical syllables (*mantras*), which are concerted into a single dynamic operation to convert the body into a grand talismanic symbol (Walker 1982, 44).

There are a variety of paramudras, each organized to invoke a powerful constellation of forces and assembled for a particular purpose. "... such practices are extremely complex [and] are never fully described in writing, being very dangerous to execute. Some are only hinted at, and not even named" (Walker 1982, 45).

Guru and Initiation: The Dynamic Link

Tantra transforms secrecy into a devotional exercise. Many of the deepest tantric secrets are not written down at all. Many of those that are written down are described in language that is deliberately made confusing, ambiguous, and obscure.

For that reason alone, the guru, or spiritual master, is essential to the survival and transmission of the tantric tradition. The function of the guru is to reveal to the disciple the secret practices and teachings, and the secret meanings of the scriptures. But the guru has a deeper function, as well. He (or she) is also considered a vehicle for the secret spiritual dynamism of the tradition itself.

> The guru is the living flame, and he alone can charge the unlit wick of the pupil (*chela*), duly dipped in the oil of cultic teachings, with the divine light. Practical initiation is impossible without a guru (Walker 1982, 26).

The initiation ritual is seen as the living connection between the disciple and the spiritual power of the tradition embodied in the guru. The ritual is known as *diksha* (enhallowment) and varies in detail according to the tradition of the guru and the level of initiation being conducted. Normally, however, an entry-level diksha will include the following elements: worship of the guru; conveying of spiritual power from guru to disciple, usually in the form of a "seed mantra"; instructions for using the mantra; and instructions for visualization meditations.

> Finally, he is given the name and details of his own personal deity . . . generally a particular facet, or personified power aspect of one of the major deities of the sect. . . . The chela now has a formula for repetition, a ritual for practice, and a deity for personal worship (Walker 1981, 27).

Maithuna: Sex as Worship

The sexual ritual automatically commands the center of attention in any discussion of tantra, and thus it is easy to distort or misunderstand its real place in tantric practice.

145

The ritual is known as *maithuna*. Even in those tantric sects that advocate its literal enactment, the rite itself is reserved for experienced practitioners. It contains a number of individual elements, each requiring its own form of training. Only after sufficient preparation can they all be drawn together in a carefully coordinated series of exercises that turn the tantric's body into a clearinghouse of interdimensional energies.

Almost all tantric traditions emphasize that physical release through orgasm and ejaculation is *not* the objective of mai-thuna. The tantric objective is quite the opposite. By the particular combination of exercises that constitute the ritual, the practitioner seeks to achieve the "three-fold immobility" of semen, breath, and consciousness. When arousal is arrested at the point of maximum tension, when breathing ceases and mind is in a state of still, but focused, receptivity, then the tantric transcendence takes place. The restraint of release on the physical level closes the valve on its normal channel of discharge. Maithuna stimulates, then traps the energies of erotic arousal and finally releases them through the channel of the "still mind," that is, in a transcendent, "spiritual" orgasm that fuses the tantric's own inner polarities in union with the One.

Lefthand/Righthand: Tantric Dialectic

Insofar as *maithuna* provides a practical experience of One-ness, it is the foundation of higher tantric practices. But there is considerable division between tantrics on whether *maithuna* should be understood as a literal act performed concretely as described in tantric texts or as eroticized symbolism for higher mental states.

Tantrics are designated as "lefthand" or "righthand," depending on whether they interpret the *maithuna* passages literally or figuratively. Righthand tantrics (also called white tantrics) interpret the passages figuratively. Lefthand tantrics (also called red tantrics) take the instructions literally and in fact engage in concrete sexual acts in their ritual performances.

146

The Language of the Twilight Zone

Without doubt, the chief obstacle to understanding tantra is the matter of tantric language. We have already seen that tantra assaults language in its use of *mantra*. In this form, language is stripped of its function as an agent of meaning and communication and instead becomes the agent of fusion, a state in which communication is meaningless and meaning is inconceivable.

Mantra is just one manifestation of tantra's corrosion of meaning, and a minor one, at that. More generally, the tantric scriptures display an ambiguous style of language that is called *sandha-bhasa*. Tantric texts are often composed in: "a secret, dark, ambiguous language in which a state of consciousness is expressed by an erotic term and the vocabulary of mythology or cosmology is charged with Hatha-yogic or sexual meanings" (Eliade 1969, 249).

The language of the tantras is the language of the twilight zone: A form of usage in which various meanings flow together, intersect, and branch out in a hundred different implications.

There appear to be two basic reasons for tantra's extensive reliance on what could be called the "language of mutable meaning."

The first is disguise and misdirection. The mutable style serves to camouflage the thrust of tantric instruction; it hides the truths of tantra from orthodox rivals and from the profane curiosity of the uninitiated. Those it cannot mislead, it confuses.

Only the tantric disciple holds the key to sandha-bhasa and can correctly decipher the puzzles it presents. But even for the initiate, sandha-bhasa serves a function of deliberate confusion. The mutable mode is precisely designed . . .

> to project the yogin into the "paradoxical situation" indispensable to his training. The semantic polyvalence of words finally substitutes ambiguity for the usual system of reference inherent in every ordinary language. And this destruction of language contrib-

147

utes in its own way, too, toward "breaking" the profane universe and replacing it by a universe of convertible and integrable planes (Eliade 1969, 250–251).

In this context, the multiple semantic structure of sandha-bhasa is the linguistic equivalent of occult correspondence. It has the same effect on language that tantra in general has on reality: It first fragments it, then diffuses it, and finally dissolves it.

Tantra vs. Existence

In this we glimpse tantra's underlying spiritual dynamism: its fundamental adversity to the creation, humanity, and human nature. Every level of tantric practice constitutes an assault on the realm of normal experience by literally disintegrating it—by dissolving it into its occult (hidden) components, then using those elemental forces of creation as links to forces that are beyond creation altogether. Tantra unravels the normal world of perception and understanding and reweaves it into an intricate network of occult correspondences that ultimately vanishes into the One. This is the condition that the tantric seeks, and it is patently the doorway to dissolution. Tantra is how the world looks as it disappears.

Tantra and Christianity

Christianity and tantra face each other as virtual mirror images. Each system exalts what the other devalues and affirms what the other denies. Therefore, analysis of tantra from a Christian viewpoint (or vice versa) offers almost limitless possibilities for comment. There are far too many avenues of comparison to explore in an article of this length. Therefore, I would like to conclude with a summary contrast of tantra and Christianity on a matter that is fundamental to both: the nature of existence and humanity.

148

In tantra, perfection is the undisturbed self-awareness of the One, but this perfect bliss is spoiled by its descent into duality, manifestation, and illusion. In tantra, god goes wrong, while humanity and the universe suffer the consequences on his behalf, in the misery and alienation of existence. God has his lila, but we get the *karma*.

In Christianity, God creates a perfect world He declares superbly good, but this excellent handiwork is spoiled by the descent of its stewards into sin and disobedience. In Christianity, humanity and the universe go wrong, while God suffers the consequences on our behalf in the agony and alienation of the crucifixion. "Though we were yet sinners, Christ died for us."

In that set of inverted images, we find the final subjective appeal of tantra to fallen human beings of this age or any other. Tantra makes humanity into an innocent victim of its own condition and fixes responsibility for the state of things on incredibly ancient tremors of impersonal consciousness. It is a roundabout route to pinning the Fall on God.

Thus tantric teaching functions effectively to relieve the psychospiritual pressure of sin and guilt. Tantric practice and the tantric experience of "salvation" powerfully reinforce that effect. The tantric's "transcendence" into the One dissolves human identity deliberately and permanently. For the personal soul, as a means of dealing with conscience, guilt, and judgment, it is the ultimate vanishing act: There is no one to be judged, if there is no one at all!

Adam and Eve's first response to God's presence after their disobedience was to hide, to conceal themselves by blending in among the rest of the creation.

> And they heard the sound of the Lord God walking in the garden in the cool of the day, and the man and his wife hid themselves from the presence of the Lord God among the trees of the garden (*see* Genesis 3:8, 9).

This universal, distinctively fallen, and very human impulse is expressed in many ways, as most of us know all too well. But tantra gives the tendency a status that is radical, paradoxical, and unique. Tantra takes the "natural" response to the pressure of sin and guilt—i.e., concealment and disappearance—and enshrines it as an ultimate standard of truth. Tantra accepts this primal reaction of fallen humanity, amplifies it, then consecrates it as a tool for extinguishing human existence. Tantra exalts and intensifies the energies of human fallenness precisely so as to use those energies as an instrument to dismember human nature. The desire to hide becomes the will to self-destruct.

Tantra makes final the fallenness of the world. It takes the world as human experience receives it, in its fallenness, and seals it into a self-contained system that holds out ultimate dissolution as the proper end of all things.

Tantra gleams like a talisman of truth, but its truth is death, and its gloss is pure, refined hubris.

Tantra in the West

Marco Polo virtually set our image of Asia in concrete. Since his time (d. 1324), the West has seen the East as a fabulous realm of wealth and wonder. Many of the earliest Europeans to probe the East traveled there explicitly in search of esoteric learning. Some returned to Europe with the claim of occult powers, and developed reputations to support it. These flamboyant characters provided the earliest implanting of Oriental occultism within European culture.

> Foremost among them were: the semi-legendary Christian Rosenkreuz (d. 1484) who visited . . . the Middle East, and returned to Germany to set up the Rosicrucian fraternity; the celebrated Swiss-German alchemist and occultist Theophrastus Paracelsus (d. 1541), who allegedly visited the Cham of Tartary; the

enigmatic comte de Saint-Germain (d. 1784) who was said to have travelled to India and learnt Sanskrit; Count Alessandro di Cagliostro (d. 1795), founder of an influential masonic order, who spent many years in the Orient (Walker 1981, 104).

From the earliest days, the occult West and the esoteric East have remained in intimate relationship and close communication. Almost all forms of occult teaching make direct use of Eastern philosophical notions. The image of the East in Western occultism borrows heavily from tantric lore, especially where the emphasis is on mystical powers and magical abilities.

Though tantra was in Western occultism, it was part of a closed world. Those who were affected by tantra were those who came into the world of occultism, not those outside it.

The Advent of the Western Adept

The East began to attract the interest of serious men of learning as Western trade expanded into Asia during the seventeenth century. Within a century, the great Orientalists of Britain, France, and Germany had begun their pioneering work of bringing the Eastern scriptures to the Western reading public. Much of their labors consisted of translation and commentary, but few of them visited the Orient in person.

In time, articulate, educated Westerners arose, who steeped themselves in Oriental culture and consciously functioned as apostles of tantric knowledge to the West. One of the first and most influential was Sir John Woodroffe, a British colonial magistrate in eastern India at the beginning of this century.

Most recently, Westerners have pursued tantrism in increasing numbers. Some, such as the Europeans Aghananda Bharati (Indian tantra) and Lama Anagarika Govinda (Tibetan Buddhism), have contributed greatly to our knowledge of tantra. Other Westerners have signed up with traditional tantric gurus as disciples, public-relations people, or teachers and initiators.

Still others, like the American Ram Dass (Richard Alpert), have become pop gurus, conveying tantric ideas on a mass scale through lectures, books, and movies.

The Coming of the Swamis

Tantra has also imported itself to Western shores in the form of guru-based religious cults, mostly of Indian origin. The surprising fact is that most of the Indian gurus in the West have been delivering tantra, whatever they may be advertising. Aagaard singles out the divine role of the guru and the presence of kundalini practices as tests of tantric influence.

Swami Vivekananda led the thrust of Eastern religions into the Western mind, just before the turn of the century. A disciple of the well-known Swami Ramakrishna, Vivekananda established the Vedanta Society, a missionary arm of neo-Hinduism. Both Ramakrishna and Vivekananda were tantrists (Aagaard 1980, 7). Swami Yogananda was another early exponent of Hindu spirituality in America. Yogananda wrote the popular and influential *Autobiography of a Yogi* and founded the Self-Realization Fellowship in the United States during the 1930s. Yogananda's spiritual lineage has a direct tantric link. His own guru's guru was "Lahiri Mahasaya, one of the most important gurus in the Tantric renaissance of the last century" (Aagaard 1980, 10).

The Transcendental Meditation (TM) of Maharishi Mahesh Yogi is likewise a form of tantric teaching that has been heavily sanitized for public presentation.

The Divine Light Mission (DLM) is another group with tantric roots that are deep but not obvious. Again, the first clue is the extravagant emphasis given to the divinity of the guru. The DLM is, in fact, a form of truncated tantra which exclusively emphasizes the top three chakras and uses a limited range of techniques.

Some gurus are more openly tantric. Two of these who plainly state their case are Swami Muktananda and Bhagwan Rajneesh.

Muktananda calls his teachings *siddha* Yoga, because he emphasizes the supernatural powers, or siddhis, which are gained by the adept. The guru worship that characterizes all tantric groups is extremely strong in the siddha Yoga tradition. By worship, one taps the guru's power, and the guru can transmit his power by a touch, or even a glance. This is called *shaktipat*.

Muktananda was first brought to this country by Werner Erhard of *est*, and Muktananda returned the favor by making a substantial contribution to Erhard's philosophy. It is reasonable to assume that he gave Werner *shaktipat* as well.

Many more groups and gurus are tantric in orientation, although as Aagaard says, "most gurus explicitly deny their own tantric roots." No doubt they wish to evade the taint of tantra's still seamy reputation. Whatever the reason, the result has been that most gurus are teaching basic aspects of tantra without identifying it as such. Thus tantra's impact in the West has been enormous, but covert. Our fascination with Eastern spirituality in general has been a fascination with tantra in particular, whether we knew it or not.

Chemical Bliss, the Occult, and the Counterculture

The twentieth century's rising interest in Eastern religions has been paralleled by a rising occult interest. The occult revival of the 1960s brought occult notions to the forefront of popular attention. In doing so, it drew from several important sources that had been established decades earlier. Chief among them were theosophy, Gurdjieff, Aleister Crowley, and the Ordo Templi Orientis (O.T.O.). All of these were heavily influenced by tantra. One of Crowley's friends allegedly revealed the O.T.O.'s highest secrets of sex-magic to L. Ron Hubbard, founder of Scientology (Walker 1981, 111).

The use of drugs naturally linked the counterculture with the occult and also with tantra, especially lefthand tantra. Many tantric scriptures endorse marijuana and other mind-altering drugs as a legitimate form of spiritual practice.

The LSD of counterculture fame produced extraordinary experiences that did not come with an attached interpretation. Early experimenters with LSD looked around for some expertise at interpreting drug states, and they found tantra. Timothy Leary, Ralph Metzner, and Richard Alpert used themes of mystical illumination to understand the LSD experience. Their final interpretation of the "psychedelic experience" was published in 1964 as a commentary on the *Tibetan Book of the Dead,* an important tantric scripture.

Thus the tantric slant of the counterculture was nailed down from the beginning. Tantric themes showed up throughout the counterculture. Almost anything that was said about sex, drugs, or enlightenment contained implicit tantric assumptions. In particular, the counterculture's art and music, the most potent and universal of its influences, are filled with tantric concepts and imagery. Couched in the metaphor of an inner mounting flame, the sexually oriented message of "Light My Fire," by Jim Morrison and the Doors, is an excellent example. Other instances could be chosen at random.

The Fall of Tibet

When Tibet was occupied and then annexed by the Chinese in the late 1950s, the Dalai Lama and thousands of the Buddhist religious establishment took refuge in India. Some of Tibet's spiritual and intellectual elite subsequently migrated to the West. They came to Western Europe first, and reached America about a decade after their original flight and exile.

Tarthang Tulku came to America in 1969 and founded a meditation center in Berkeley. In 1970 Chogyam Trungpa arrived; one center had already been started in Vermont by a group of his former students from Scotland, and later in 1970 another was founded in Colorado (Anderson 1979, 4).

It is hard to grasp the importance of the Tibetan upheaval. The impact of Tibet on the West can be seen, but it has not yet been measured. Nor has the impact of the West upon Tibet.

> This brings us to the intriguing question of what form Buddhism is likely to take in the United States, what native shamanism of our own it is likely to merge with. . . . As it happens, we have any number of contemporary social and intellectual movements that are marching in roughly the same direction as Tibetan Buddhism. It is amazing how closely this ancient religion parallels humanistic psychology . . . (Anderson 1979, 15–16).

Anderson (1979) notes that different aspects of Buddhist tantra are compatible with the human-potential movement, Western phenomenology, Jungian psychology, modern theoretical physics, and the environmental movement.

Hollywood Hindus

At all levels, tantra continues to get ever-wider exposure. In *Indiana Jones and the Temple of Doom*, the hero combats a lefthand tantric sect for possession of a primeval *shiva-lingam* (the film's fictitious "shankara stone"). He succeeds, and returns the tantric talisman to its rightful possessors, presumably a righthand sect which uses the talisman in a benign and "natural" way. Suddenly, as of 1984, millions of Americans have been introduced to tantra for the price of a theater ticket.

Secularizing Tantra

The story of tantra in the West is just beginning. Tantrism will undoubtedly continue to get wider publicity and more

adherents through traditional avenues. But tantra's main channel of influence for the future will be through secularized forms
of its teaching.

As Westerners have recently encountered tantra and become
tantric initiates in numbers, they have done their typically
secular thing: They appropriated traditional knowledge as a
tool for the autonomous will. In the process, they discarded
those portions of tradition that interfered with that purpose or
simply did not appeal to them.

To many Western tantrics, this attitude means that tantric
secrets can be revealed apart from the traditional structure of
guru and initiation. When this attitude is combined with the
means of mass communication that exist in the West, pop
tantra emerges. As a result, tantra is cut off from its tradition—
not in terms of content, which can be conveyed by the printed
page, but in terms of control, which cannot.

Several recent books introduce the reader to tantric theory,
practice, and secrets in greater or lesser detail. One example is
a Bantam mass-market paperback (1969), entitled *Sex and
Yoga*, by Nancy Phelan and Michael Volin. In 160 pages it
gives a simplified version of tantric cosmology, psychology,
and spirituality, including the concept of enlightenment and
self-divinization. It prescribes a regime of tantric exercises
specifically intended to strengthen and purify different parts
of the body related to the sexual function. Price: ninety-five
cents.

A more recent, more flagrant, and more expensive instance
is *Sexual Secrets: The Alchemy of Ecstacy*, by Nik Douglas
and Penny Slinger (1979). This is much more than a summary
tour of tantric thought with a sprinkling of basic exercises.
Sexual Secrets weighs in with 383 profusely illustrated pages
and a price tag of $14.95. Within those pages is a thorough
elaboration of the tantric worldview, as well as detailed
instructions for almost the entire range of basic tantric
practices. In addition, there are voluminous instructions on
the details of intercourse and erotic practices in general. The

authors are tantric initiates and claim extensive training under Eastern adepts.

Douglas and Slinger clearly represent the viewpoint of lefthand tantra, and they plead their cause quite openly. At least there is no twilight language here:

> By exploring the sexual potential of ourselves and others, we can come to consciously know the alchemy of ecstacy. . . . This is a book for those who wish to use the sexual bond as a means to liberation and who desire to transcend the limits of the individual self (Douglas and Slinger 1970, 12).

8

PERSONAL GROWTH: FINDING OR LOSING THE SELF

Karen C. Hoyt

A STUDENT OF SILVA MIND CONTROL RELAYS HER EXPERIENCE:

She put down the phone and concentrated. It took only a moment to get down to her levels and use the *Screen of her Mind.*

She had the name, address, and the age. She apparently needed no more. She saw a woman with pale blue eyes and dark brown hair, quite incongruous for her years, and she knew with sudden conviction that she had locked into the right person.

"I put a light around her eyes and saw what I assumed to be cataracts drop away. I had the feeling, as remarkable as it was, that she was cured."

Three days later she got a second call from Hazel

Wightt's friend. "It's a miracle!" he exclaimed. "Hazel can see again, and she is eternally grateful" (Stearn, 1976, 31).

The following is a condensed version of *est*'s "Affirmation of Life," which was read to participants while they were in a state of deep relaxation (as remembered by a participant):

> My sense of awareness and my mind are developing so that I am becoming able to project my consciousness into any space at any time on this planet, any planet in the solar system in the galaxy, any galaxy in the universe; and I am becoming able to be aware of what exists and what is happening at any time when this is done ethically. My sense of my awareness and my mind is developing the willingness and openness so that I am becoming able to project my consciousness into the different grounds of the universe, one of its bases, into the vegetable kingdom and any one of its bases, into the animal kingdom and any one of its bases, and the human body, and finally into the mind and any one of its bases.

American Health magazine (Clifford 1987) describes Shirley MacLaine's mystical experience in the Andes:

> In MacLaine's description, her "spirit, or mind, or soul, whatever it was" flowed out of her body—though the two were connected by a "thin, thin silver cord." She says she floated so high she could "see" the Earth's curvature. "I was just flowing, somehow flowing. I didn't want to return, which made me question whether I'd gone too far, and that was enough to take me back ... Then, well, I just became 130 pounds again."

Silva mind control, Werner Erhart's *est*, and Shirley Mac-Laine's psychic adventures are examples of the many-faceted New Age movement.

Is the New Age movement simply another method of self-help in America's pluralistic society, or is it psychopathology with a religious or psychological gloss? The New Age movement forces us to reevaluate what it means to be human. It claims to push back the former limits of man's finiteness and to open up a whole new horizon of consciousness and power that previously has been reserved for God.

Does this new paradigm reveal the true nature of man, or is it a grand delusion?

The New Age movement's worldview is one of undifferentiated oneness, where the mind and consciousness are the primary reality. In this state there is no good or evil. You are not limited by your body, your sex, your mind, or your abilities.

According to NAM, humanity is on the threshold of a major evolutionary leap forward, a transformation of radical dimensions. This transformation will propel us onto a much higher spiritual plane which includes an awareness of our godhood or goddesshood.

According to the Judeo-Christian worldview, man is separate, is limited in his power and knowledge, is limited to space and time, is rooted in material reality, is capable of rationality as well as emotions, and is constrained by laws and a moral sense of good and evil, with clear sexual taboos. In short, we are just ordinary mortals.

When we begin to talk about pathology, we must first address what is normal. And this is exactly where the problem begins, because the New Age view of man and normality is radically different from the Judeo-Christian concept of normal. The worldview we subscribe to makes a distinct difference in our view of psychology and pathology.

The New Age movement is made up of many different groups. Although these groups hold a common metaphysic, they vary widely in their structure, sophistication, approaches, emphases, and beliefs. Some are small support groups with no hierarchy and a great deal of flexibility and diversity. Others are highly structured and highly authoritarian. Some groups seem to focus on self-help, while others have as their goal the transformation of the world. In short, there is as much diversity within the New Age movement as there is within Christianity.

It is important not to generalize from one group to another. What may be true of George Leonard may or may not be true of Silva Mind Control or Shirley MacLaine.

Among the different types of groups within the New Age movement are:

1. Self-help training groups
2. Psychic groups, mind reading, healing, prophecy
3. Spiritism and channeling
4. Eastern religious groups

With few exceptions, all New Age groups subscribe to a common view of humanity, summarized below. Following the New Age view are mental health implications. (For a full comparison of the biblical and New Age world views, see the compete chart in the Appendix.)

New Age World View: The emanations of god—the cosmos—are appearances which have only limited and deceptive reality. The cosmos is therefore *maya*, the play of illusion.
Implication: What appears real is an illusion.

New Age World View: Humanity is not distinct from god. Like ultimate reality, they are reducible to pure energy, light, or consciousness, featureless and impersonal.
Implication: Man is god . . . There is no separate personal self.

New Age World View: Human beings have no innate attributes and no inherent limitations. All options are open. Human beings inherently embody all the power, knowledge, and wisdom of the cosmos, as well as its divine nature.

Implication: Man has unlimited potential . . . Man has god's abilities and the potential to be omniscient, omnipotent, and sovereign.

New Age World View: Death is the final stage of growth.
Implication: Death is an illusion.

New Age World View: The dilemma of humanity is a constriction of awareness. We have limited our consciousness so we do not perceive the One, but only fragments of it.
Implication: Humanity's real problems are denied and seen as ultimately illusionary.

New Age World View: From birth we are taught to break reality up into parts and pieces. The categories of good and bad, us and them, me and you, are barriers to true perception of the One. Then, in addition, those who teach the primacy of reason and belief hinder the experience of full consciousness and therefore the advent of the New Age.
Implication: With no psychological or moral distinctions, there is no basis for a personal or social self. Reason, belief, and logic are discouraged. Altered states are encouraged.

New Age World View: All the hatred and misery we see around us derives from the simple error of attributing reality to separate, limited, individual existence.
Implication: Separateness is an illusion. Separateness is bad. Negative emotions are seen as the problem and are to be avoided.

This leads us to eight areas that bear closer inspection.

New Age Movement	Psychological Worldview (Human developmental necessities)
1. No distinctions; no ego boundaries	1. Distinctions and ego boundaries
2. Cause and effect as a result of mind, not actions	2. Cause and effect via actions and behavior
3. Fusion and union sought	3. Separation, individuation sought
4. Reality is an illusion	4. General reliability of sense perceptions
5. Emotions over the rational; image over language	5. Equality of the rational and emotional. Importance of consensual language for communication
6. We are gods	6. We are ordinary mortals
7. There is no good and evil	7. There is good and evil
8. No sexual boundaries	8. Incest taboos, sexual distinctions

Let's examine these in more detail.

Distinctions

Making distinctions is crucial to becoming a functional adult. Without the ability to make distinctions, a person's world remains a primal chaos. Among the basic types of distinctions we need to make are:

1. The distinction between what is "me" and what is not "me"
2. The distinction among different kinds of emotions
3. The distinction between objective and subjective
4. The distinction that people are different from animals, rocks, trees, or God
5. The relational distinction ("I am physically and psychically separate from others.")
6. The distinction between fantasy, or make-believe, and reality
7. The sexual distinction ("I am a boy" or "I am a girl")

Only as distinctions are made can a real self-image be gained.

The New Age view is that distinctions are neither good nor helpful, but rather that they keep us from the realization that we are one with all people, the cosmos, and God. The NAM sees these distinctions—these boundaries—as a major cause of our miseries. In his book *No Boundary* (1981), Ken Wilbur focuses on this issue:

> We artificially split our awareness into compartments such as subject vs. object, life vs. death, mind vs. body, inside vs. outside, reason vs. instinct—a divorce settlement that sets experience cutting into experience and life fighting with life. The result of such violence . . . is simply unhappiness. Life becomes suffering, full of battles. But all of the battles in our experience—our conflicts, anxieties, sufferings and despairs—are created by the boundaries we misguidedly throw around our experience.

The New Age movement does not accept ontological distinctions; to them, there is no difference in being between a rock and a flower. Ontological merger makes it impossible to distinguish between fantasy and reality. Even a young child knows that Donald Duck is make-believe and not human. An inability to make this distinction is animism: the belief that inert objects are living and have consciousness. This type of merger is sought by the NAM. An illustration of ontological blurring appeared in a healer's ad in *Common Ground* (1986):

> Today many people feel separate or alone. Yet you can learn how to connect with your environment and the love within you and around you by establishing, harmonizing and becoming more aware of your connection to plants, animals, cars, Xerox machines, sunsets, etc. Having the environment as peer-peer, student-teaching . . . and expanding your love.

In contrast, from a developmental psychological view, the ability to make distinctions is both necessary and good. While a sophisticated New Ager might argue that making distinctions is not inherently bad or may even be essential for functioning, he would say it is inherently arbitrary, relative, and artificial.

Cause and Effect

You, my beloved brethren, are the cause of your creation, all of it. It is your own dream you are living, it is your own reality you are acting out on this stage of life. How will you come to know all there is to know? Accept what you are, take responsibility for all you have created. Love yourself. Feel joy and allow, allow, allow!! (Knight 1986.) [J. Z. Knight is the purported channel for Ramatha, a 35,000-year-old entity.]

The infant and young child have a primitive concept of cause and effect that is highly subjective and egocentrically overinclusive. The child believes his wishing or wanting causes all things. He is hungry and wishes to be fed; the bottle or breast appears. He experiences; "When I am hungry, I am fed. Mother is there. I feel good. The world is good." Conversely, when he is hungry and mother is not there, he feels: "I feel bad. The world is bad," or "Others are bad and hurting me."

The natural infantile worldview is that our thinking, wishing, or feeling *causes* things to happen. The child must be helped to understand it is his *behavior*, not his wish, that has an effect on the external world, and that things happen without his influence. He must learn that his power is limited.

Egocentric cause and effect develop from the primitive, infantile belief that thinking or wishing something will make it happen, which is, in effect, a belief in magic. The child, not having adequate experience to interpret and explain life's events, creates stories to give events meaning and order. He may believe these stories to be true. The parents mitigate the child's fanciful world by explaining the true causes of life's events, so the child can learn the difference between his stories (as wonderful or scary as they may be) and reality. If the parents do not have this clear in their own minds, they cannot help the child mature out of this stage, and the child may stay stuck in this magical, egocentrical view of the universe.

This egocentricity carries with it the feelings of omnipotence, power, and grandiosity, and has both positive and negative aspects. You become responsible for all the good that occurs, but also for all the bad. This is a source for primitive guilt; you are responsible when anything bad happens, or even if anyone feels bad.

The New Age movement appears to hold onto the belief in egocentric cause and effect—holding that the wish (referred to as "higher" or "cosmic consciousness") causes reality to change. *Est* is one of the NAM groups that is best known for this. A participant talks about being "at cause" and responsibility (participant names are not revealed to assure confidentiality):

> The trainer was discussing total responsibility, and I became confused and upset by his reference to our having everything we wanted in our life—we created it this way. I am diabetic and had to sit in the last row of chairs in the room because I needed to eat at times. This row of trainees was referred to as "the victims." When I raised my hand to question the total-responsibility concept, the trainer said of course I had trouble accepting it—I'm sitting in the victim row. He asked why I sat there. When he heard the reason, he asked me to tell him something about my childhood. I told him I felt that my father rejected me as a child. He then said I created my diabetes to get attention from and to control and manipulate my father, and that I continued to use it for those reasons. He suggested that I fantasized as a child about getting various illnesses to "show my father." He was correct in that, so I thought there may be some validity to his assertion. However, I was very upset.

She goes on to talk about the conflict this created in dealing with her first marriage:

At the time, I became extremely confused, and issues I had worked on in counseling and in support groups—concerning my first marriage and how I needed to end it in order to get myself and my children healthy, since my husband wasn't willing to get help—all came rushing to the surface and became confused with "I created him that way—I'm responsible for it all." I think my defense mechanism was just to sit down and accept everything else in training.

The Hunger Project, while it denies any formal connection with *est* or Werner Erhard, takes the concept of "at cause" to its next logical step. They believe they can affect the world through changing group consciousness. Their method is to sign up people to commit (will?) themselves to the end of hunger. In 1985, they raised six million dollars. Only three percent of it actually went for development or food for needy people; the rest was focused toward changing people's attitudes and consciousnesses about hunger (5th Estate, 1986). The project teaches that if enough people believe the time has come for hunger to end, that belief can actually end hunger.

This approach is built on the belief that our desires, wishes, and thinking are not confined to our bodies, rather, all is consciousness, all is mind; events and objects are projections of the mind and have no true existence of their own, apart from our minds. To want it is to create it. This is positive thinking in the extreme. From a psychological viewpoint, it is egocentric cause and effect; it is magic.

Is There a Personal Self?

The goal of growing up is to establish a personal self, separate and autonomous from others. To leave the symbiotic union with the mother and come to grips with one's separate self is one of life's key challenges. Judith Viorst expresses this struggle well in her best-seller, *Necessary Losses* (1986, 34):

All of our loss experiences hark back to Original Loss; the loss of that ultimate mother-child connection. For before we begin to encounter the inevitable separations of everyday life, we live in a state of oneness with our mother. This ideal state, this state of boundarylessness, this I-am-you-are-me-is-she-is-we, this "harmonious interpenetrating mix-up," this floating "I'm alone in the milk and the milk's in me," this chillproof insulation from aloneness and intimations of mortality: This is a condition known to lovers, saints, psychotics, druggies and infants. It is called bliss.

Giving up this interconnectedness so we can grow is the premise of Viorst's *Necessary Losses*. If we don't, we stay immature and create a fantasy to replace the harsh demands of reality. This symbiotic union is the primary focus of NAM philosophy.

Ken Wilber explains, in *No Boundary* (1981, 3):

> The most fascinating aspect of such awesome and illuminating experiences—and the aspect to which we will be devoting much attention—is that the individual comes to feel, beyond any shadow of a doubt, that he is fundamentally one with the entire universe, with all worlds, high or low, sacred or profane. His *sense of identity* expands far beyond the narrow confines of his mind and body and embraces the entire cosmos.

NAM's goal is union (A fantasy reunion with the mother, I believe). In the process, the self is lost, given up to become one with the longed-for maternal object.

The NAM view of self is described by Werner Erhard (Bartley 1978, 181):

> We know, for instance, that there is nothing per-
> sonal about Self; that it is misleading to speak to my
> Self. The Self is beyond any individual, identifica-
> tion, form process, or position—and gives rise to
> them. Nor is the Self "conscience" or (as in Scien-
> tology) some immortal spirit that resides within
> individuals. No position, the Self is the space or
> context in which all positionality in life occurs. No
> thing, the Self is the space of things. It contains the
> "screen of life" but never appears upon it.

For Erhard, there is no personal self (small s), but rather only the universal Self.

Not to move on developmentally—not to separate and de-velop a personal, real self—is pathological, according to devel-opmental psychology. Psychiatrist James F. Masterson (1980) depicts four psychological stages of early development between birth and the age of thirty-six months:

1. Autistic: The infant experiences self and mother as one unit: There are no distinctions.
2. Symbiotic: The mother and child are still one unit, but there are two subunits: a good, pleasure-producing unit, and a bad, frustrating unit. Each is either all good or all bad.
3. Separation/individuation: The realization comes that the self and mother are physically and psychically separate. Now the good self or the bad self and the good mother or the bad mother are experienced as separate.
4. Whole-object representation: The child sees himself as both good and bad and the mother as both good and bad. The child knows he or she is physically and psychically separate from the mother.

The New Age movement appears to make the goal of life the return to the good symbiotic unit which is a second stage of human development. But to make symbiosis the goal of your life is to regress or remain fixated at an early stage of develop-ment. With this regression comes a constellation of ego effects:

1. Poor reality perception
2. Poor frustration tolerance
3. Poor impulse control
4. Fluid ego boundaries

Thus, the New Age movement aims to have its followers return to the second of Masterson's stages of human development.

Individuals who have borderline personality disorders* often have problems outgrowing this stage of development. They believe that if they are separate—if they don't merge with the good parent—they will not be able to survive. These individuals look for an idealized leader, parent, lover, guru, or therapist with whom to merge. Their desire to merge is intense, because they have no sense of a personal self. If they cannot find a person with whom to merge, they may escape their anxiety in merger with substances such as food, alcohol, drugs, or experiences such as sex, mysticism, or altered states. Thus the New Age movement not only encourages borderline personality disorders, it also offers its followers support for the very problems it helps create in them.

Can You Trust Your Senses?

This is taken for granted in the literature of developmental psychology. The child relies on his ears, mouth, eyes, and fingers to learn about the world. If a child cannot rely on one of these senses, it usually indicates a problem with his hearing or sight. Emotionally speaking, it takes massive denial to negate

---

* "Borderline disorders represent a spectrum of disorders between psychosis and neurosis. At the lower end of the spectrum are schizotypal personality disorders which may include the following characteristics: odd communication, suspiciousness, magical thinking, undue social anxiety, and social isolation. At the higher level, toward the border of neurosis are the borderline personality disorders which may include: identity disturbance, a pattern of unstable interpersonal relationships, impulsivity or unpredictability, lack of control of anger, chronic feelings of emptiness or boredom, physically self-damaging acts" (American Psychiatric Assoc., 1980).

sense perception, or it could indicate the actual presence of hallucinations or illusions. In other words, when we cannot rely on our sense perceptions, we are either mentally or physically ill. In this state, we cannot distinguish between what is coming in through our senses and what is manufactured by our mind.

The New Age movement suggests that what we see is not really there, except in a conditional, contingent sense. Reality is an illusion, a product of our mind. They maintain that our sense perceptions are not reliable and the "out there" is not really there—at least not as we have come to believe it is. What is more profoundly *there* is spiritual, part of the universal mind, or "one," and can only be "seen" if we are in an altered state of consciousness.

Is Logical Thinking Important?

The infant moves away from emotionally connected images and ideas, to logical thinking, which gives him the ability to reason and interact with the external world.

Theodore Lidz (1973, 53) explains:

> [Without] the meanings and logic of his culture, no relationships beyond infantile dependency and no collaborative interactions with others are possible. The schizophrenic patient escapes from irreconcilable dilemmas and unbearable hopelessness by breaking through these confines to find some living space by using his own idiosyncratic meanings and reasoning, but in so doing impairs his ego functioning and ability to collaborate with others.

Personal meaning and emotions are prized by the New Age movement over and above logical thinking and shared meaning. In some groups, this means giving oneself over to intense feeling and emotion. In other groups, it is an esoteric system of images, symbols, and archetypes. But in all, emotion is prized over intellect. The intellect and reason are believed to create blocks to altered states and to hinder full consciousness.

Are We God or Ordinary Mortals?

An ordinary mortal? What a disappointment! In the ordinary mortal, wisdom must be learned. Achievements must be brought about by action, not by wishes. Praise and acceptance must be earned. There is precious little unconditional love and adoration available to adults.

The New Age movement provides the answer to this narcissistic wound. It tells us that we are God, we are perfect, and we naturally possess all knowledge and wisdom. All we need to do is come to the passive knowledge of our godliness, for God is within us, and no work is necessary. The way this is achieved is by learning a few simple techniques; it may take as little as fifteen minutes of meditation a day.

J. Z. Knight (1986, 8) gives Ramtha's message on this subject:

> The greatest and most important reason that I am here and you are here is to learn who you are and what you are. What you are is god and once you have embraced that, you embrace love; and when you know love, you become a Christ; and when you become a Christ, you become a light unto the whole of the world. When the light shines forth, the consciousness is raised; and when the consciousness is raised, it eases into superconsciousness; and when superconsciousness is upon the land, that which is called survival, decadence of mind, body and spirit, war and pestilence, they are no more. It is finished. God is. That is what you will learn and embrace through profound experience.

Ramtha (Knight 1986, 10) clarifies this point: "To live as god is not at all an arduous thing to do. It is simply breaking away from old habits and formulating new ones. It is getting into the habit of seeing yourself as unlimited God rather than vulnerable men."

The mental abilities that are often included in this omniscience are clairvoyance, telepathy, precognition, and psychokinesis (the mind's ability to affect matter).

Good and Evil

For New Agers, there is no objective good or evil. Rather, they believe that all judgments are learned through social conventions. Judgments are seen as divisive, fracturing the true oneness of us all. Hence, there can be no objective basis for morality or social justice. The only control is *karma*, which states that whatever you do comes around to you again. So if you want to advance in the next life, you should be a good person in this one, but the meaning of *good* is elusive and subjective. This is actually the Americanized version. In the Hindu version, the goal of life is to get off the reincarnation cycle completely and dissolve into the one, the nothingness, Nirvana.

Sexual Identity

Sexual identity is based upon a sense of whom we are like and whom we are unlike. In addition, the child learns who it is appropriate to be sexually involved with and who it is not. These are boundaries that some New Agers see as unnecessary, or even harmful.

The blurring of sexual boundaries can be viewed in two ways. There is androgeny, where the boundaries between maleness and femaleness are softened to the point of merger. This can result in a type of grandiosity and pseudoindependence that says "I am all things and all I need, and therefore I need no one else who would be external to me." Then there is the removal of all sexual taboos. George B. Leonard (1972, 201), a leading exponent of the New Age movement, explains:

The flowering of the Transformation will probably bring with it a progressive erosion of the incest taboo. This does not mean the advent of brother-sister marriages; marriage will not be the dominant factor in the new sexuality. The conventional incest taboos may fall quietly, almost unnoticed. As humanity comes closer to a true unity, a unity of being no less than of politics, sexual barriers will simply be ignored.

The sexual "act" will not be defined as separate from the rest of life. All of life will become erotic and what is erotic will become commonplace. Recognizing that all bodies are part of the same field, ultimately one, we shall not hesitate to touch what is really ourselves.

After considering these eight points, we can conclude that the teachings of the New Age movement reflect problems in psychological development. This results in psychological symptoms that include: an impaired personal self; grandiose merger experiences; idealized leaders; illusionary ideas of omnipotence and omniscience, and an egocentric view of cause and effect. When you put all of these symptoms together, it often produces difficulty in love and work relationships.

The impaired individual's way of protecting himself from pain and anxiety is to employ psychological defenses (*see* Chart A). The impaired person views himself as small and vulnerable and fears that if he is not joined with a good, powerful guru or leader, he will perish. When he is joined with the idealized leader, however, he experiences himself as all-powerful, all-wise, all-loving, and at peace. The New Age worldview and belief system resonate with and strengthen the defended self.

A Psychological Scenario

Let's trace a hypothetical case. Mr. White has a poor self-image. He thinks of himself as small, vulnerable, and helpless.

The Anxious Self

- Affect — Abandonment, depression (anger, fear, guilt, passivity, helplessness, emptiness, void), fragmentation, panic, suicidal and homicidal rage.
- Experiences others as withdrawing, angry, critical, uncaring and attacking.
- Experiences self as inadequate, weak, bad, ugly, ineffectual, dumb, sinful, an insect, etc.

The Defended Self

1. Acts out the wish for union (reunion) apothesis.
2. Splitting, denial, projective, identification.
3. Numbing: Dissociation, depersonalization and derealization.
4. Magical ideation.

- Experiences others (which they are "one" with) as approving, caring, accepting, supportive, loving, all powerful and all wise.
- Experiences self as good, passive child, unique — special/grandiose.
- Affect: Feeling good, powerful, euphoric, successful, gratified.

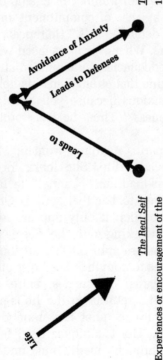

Avoidance of Anxiety

Leads to Defenses

Leads to

Life

The Real Self

- Experiences or encouragement of the real self, competence, mastery and/or assertiveness.

CHART A

The Maintenance and Defense of the Impaired Self

(The Borderline Triad)   Compiled from Masterson, J.F., 1976, 1980, 1986

He feels that if he is not joined with a good guru or the One, he will perish. When he is joined with the One—the perfect master or guru—he experiences peace.

The scenario might go something like this. Mr. White has an experience of feeling alone and helpless. This leads to anxiety. Looking for an antidote to his anxiety, he turns to meditation experiences to attain altered states of consciousness (peace). His sense of self is weakened, and in its place comes a euphoric experience that an idealized leader interprets as merger with the One. His sense of merger weakens, and as it does, he is given tasks to perform, to insure his transformation (recruit new converts, work long hours at menial tasks, repeat a certain number of chants or mantras). This in turn gives him a sense of commitment and meaning, which strengthens his "defended self." He repeats the pattern whenever anxiety occurs. Whenever he is faced with his own personal self and its inadequacies, he is immediately directed back to a New Age routine that strengthens his defended self. He is told "You feel anxious because you have given in to the illusion of separateness." Thus, he feels protected from reality.

Or consider this scenario. A young woman, Ms. Grey, is frustrated in a love relationship. She looks for a magical solution, visiting a trans-medium "channel" to find the answer. The answer is given to her that "All is One; you are god. There is no true conflict; it only appears to be a conflict because you are working out the karma from past lives." Negative emotions are split off and attributed to past lives or illusion. She tries to convince her lover of this, but if her lover does not agree, it creates more separation/individuation anxiety. She returns to the trans-medium for more advice on techniques to quiet her anxiety over being abandoned by her lover. The techniques used for this may include dissociation through meditation and/or out-of-body experiences or euphoria, as a result of intense group experiences.

In summary, then, we could say there are four basic types of responses (defenses) the New Age movement offers individuals who are suffering from anxiety.

Experiences of merger. These are designed to quiet anxiety due to feelings of separation and individuation. The merger experiences may come from idolization of the leader; trance states and meditation; use of magical substances, which might be anything from vitamins to a certain color clothing; sex, which is used particularly in tantric groups; and activities such as recruitment, selling flowers, and so forth.

Magical ideation. This gives the illusion of control and power, plus an escape from reality into fantasy. Included in this category are clairvoyance, telepathy, precognition, hypokinesis, UFOs, and past lives.

Splitting and denial. These defenses are used to deny negative emotions. Whatever is negative, in fact, can be split off and called an illusion or a hangover from an experience in a previous life. Some groups teach that there is no anger or guilt, only love. Negative emotions are caused by the individualistic ego.

Numbing (dissociation). Altered states of consciousness are taught by almost all practitioners of the New Age. These include meditation, hypnotic techniques, repetitive chanting, use of mantras, visualization exercises, and out-of-body experiences. It is believed that through these altered states, the individual can progress to higher states of consciousness. It is taught that the experiences of these altered states is true reality and the experiences of ordinary reality are an illusion.

Working together, these defense mechanisms create the illusion of feeling good, being taken care of, being nurtured, being at one, and being at peace. In addition, they are often accompanied by a euphoric sense of grandiosity, power, and wisdom.

Consider this example. Mrs. Green was concerned about her daughter Jane. Jane had become involved with a New Age group that practiced astroprojection (out-of-body experiences). The mother said, "When my daughter and I talk, if any disagreement comes up, she withdraws and says, 'Mother, you can't hurt me because I am really not here. I have left my body, and I am on the ceiling, looking down on us.' "

This is an example of depersonalization by which the individual seeks to defend herself against overwhelming anxiety. But in the New Age movement, depersonalization is raised to the level of art and ritual. Those who have spent years in one of these groups and have practiced many hours of meditation and chanting often find it impossible to come back and stay in normal reality.

Who Gets Involved in New Age?

Who gets involved in these groups? Anyone and everyone. In psychological terminology, that involves normals, borderlines, and psychotics. Each of these will find a different appeal in New Age groups.

Psychotics will see the energy—the One—the New Age talks about. They will actually become that great spirit from the past that others believe they are channeling. Reality will lose its solidity, and they will merge with the universe. Because they have no sense of self, they will lose any ability to distinguish themselves from the rest of the cosmos.

Borderlines, because of their intense idealization of a leader, will become enthusiastic recruiters and true believers. Their special vulnerability is being one with "god" or others via identification with the leader or other people in the group. However, low-level borderlines are in danger of having psychotic episodes as they try to more nearly fit the beliefs of the New Age.

Normals pick up bits and pieces of various processes, such as Yoga or TM for relaxation and stress reduction, or transformational technologies to succeed in business. They usually do not join groups or become regularly involved, unless they lead a group. Their special vulnerability is the desire to have more power, more mastery, more control.

But another important question is why and how various

people leave New Age groups. Normals simply leave after having gotten what they want or becoming dissatisfied. The exception would be if the group is a cult. (It is important to note that New Age movement groups are not necessarily cults.) Many of the New Age techniques are standard psychotherapy techniques—biofeedback, hypnosis, assertiveness training—and these techniques can be helpful to individuals in varying degrees. Most normals take the techniques that are helpful to them, discard the worldview, and leave the group once they have gotten what they can from it.

It is not so easy for the borderline to leave the group. Because New Age thinking resonates to such an extent with borderline pathology, the borderline feels as if he is leaving himself when he leaves a New Age group. When a borderline leaves, it is generally for one of three reasons: because of severe disillusionment with the leader; because his identification with the group has weakened to such an extent that abandonment depression has set in; or because (and this is particularly true of adolescents) he begins to mature, despite the group, and the emergent self comes into conflict with the structure and beliefs of the group. Usually, a borderline will move from one group to another, seeking another leader with which to identify. Seldom do they seek therapy.

The psychotic, on the other hand, does not truly ever join one of the New Age groups, because he is too odd to be accepted. However, some individuals become psychotic after they join, because of pressure brought to bear on their fragile egos and their tenuous grip on reality. Because he is an embarrassment to the group, a psychotic will usually be thrown out, although he may still seek to attach himself to the fringe of the group and practice the teachings of the group in his personal, eccentric way.

Let me give one example.

Jim had his first psychotic break while in an esoteric Eastern New Age group that emphasized godlike power and mastery via the use of meditation and certain psychospiritual tech-

niques. While in the group before his psychotic break, he was
energetic, happy, and a good student.

While Jim was a student at college, he entered an esoteric
Eastern New Age group by renting a room in one of its houses.
He felt that he was being cared for by them, living in a home
away from home, and he experienced a sense of oneness and
strength. As a result of the group's meditation practice, he
started feeling very powerful. He felt he could do anything and
have power over anyone, particularly sexual power over
women. He almost felt like a superman.

Then he fell in love with a woman who was not part of the
group, and this created a problem. He felt a disparity between
his vulnerable real self and the superman he had come to
believe he was. He told his girlfriend several of the secrets of
the group, and in so doing, felt he had committed some kind of
cosmic treason, for which he would be punished.

Consequently, he felt he had to break up with her. He
describes this experience:

> As I entered her room, she was sitting at her desk.
> A dark shadow pushed by me, and I experienced a
> great whirling wind and a fear that somebody was
> going to kill her or take her away. I shouted, "Don't
> take her, don't take her," and then offered myself,
> instead. At that time, all my power left.

Two and a half years later, I saw Jim for the first time. By this
time, he had had two hospitalizations and been diagnosed as
schizophrenic. In his early twenties, he was charming, bright,
verbal, and psychotic. He told me he felt the group had done
this to him. He felt he had lost his soul in the room that night
with his girlfriend and wondered if I could help him get it back.

Jim saw energy and auras. He experienced parts of himself—
his soul, his mind, or his body—as disconnected or numb. He
also exhibited extreme sexual-identity confusion. He wanted
me to be his girlfriend and guru, and seemed both comforted
and angry when I set limits in this area. He could not distin-

guish between thinking and doing. He resisted any talk of hospitalization.

Within the nine months I saw him, Jim dismissed three psychiatrists. He continually pushed me for the answer—the magic formula to explain his psychotic experience. He was seeking a key to put his life back together again. He felt he needed something that would produce a shock. He felt that when he went into the room with his girlfriend, he had been shocked, so all he needed now was a magic formula to "reshock" him. His example was, "If I jump off the Golden Gate Bridge, halfway down I would be shocked and understand the answer, and everything would be as it was, and I could go on with my life."

Jim finally terminated treatment when he went to a psychic and found his answer. The answer was a past life, where he and his girlfriend had been lovers. They had been in a war, a soldier had come and slit her throat. Jim had shouted, "Don't take her." He felt that working with the psychic would enable him to find the answer that would eliminate his shock experience in the girl's bedroom.

The psychic, of course, presented him with magical answers that would contain his psychosis for a while—until he once again felt stressed by the real world.

That is an example in which a psychotic breakdown was precipitated by the worldview of an all-powerful self. Originally the group had given Jim a defense that covered his very shaky adolescent sense of self. But its view of reality kept him from maturing at a speed he could manage. With this defense, he plunged into a depth of relationships for which he was unprepared.

At times as I worked with him, Jim had lucid and poignant insights into what had happened to him. He explained what being in the group was like: "I felt like a rock who had gained consciousness. I looked up and saw the birds fly and the people walking around. I wanted that, too, but then I was just a rock and would never be able to do those things."

Most New Age adherents are not like Jim. Most of them

operate with a selective suspension of belief in reality. This selectiveness enables them to function in reality while maintaining their "omnipotent" self. In order to have the experiences that the New Age promises, they have to suspend their belief in reality. But in order to function in the world, they have to believe in reality. For example, most New Agers (normals and borderlines) look both ways before crossing the street. They don't want to be hit or killed, even if the truck is illusionary and death is not real. On the other hand, a psychotic in a florid state may not look both ways, because reality is actually illusion to him.

Pathological Answers Within Christianity

It's easy to say that Christianity is the answer, but psychologically, it may not be. Within Christianity there are many fringe groups and beliefs that resonate with borderline pathology and wait with open arms for such individuals.

Let me mention a few "pathological answers" within Christianity:

1. Idealized leaders or pastors whom adherents are taught to adore, serve, and merge with
2. Groups that denounce all others as apostate and proclaim that only their special select few will bring in the kingdom of God
3. The promotion of feelings of oceanic oneness with the group or the leader, and therefore with God
4. Magic ideation—sometimes referred to as "name it, claim it, and frame it" theology. This is a magical view of prayers
5. Other types of magic are taught in some groups, by which sin can be visualized on someone's forehead, thoughts can be read, or the power to heal is automatically dispensed

Then how is orthodox Christianity different from New Age pathology? Biblical Christianity, as an antidote to the New Age movement, teaches the following:

1. Man is a separate being and is responsible for his actions.
2. Man is ontologically different from plants, animals, the cosmos, and God, and will never be God.
3. Man was created in the image of God, but is capable of evil. Hence, personal evil is real.
4. While man may experience moments of oneness and bliss, his individuality is never obliterated.
5. Things in life are accomplished through actions, not through wishes or thoughts.
6. Man is to be in relationship with others, even when those relationships are not gratifying to him.
7. There is only one God, and man does not share His omnipotence, His omniscience, His sovereignty, or His eternalness.
8. Idealization of objects or people is idolatry.
9. Conflict, pain, struggle, and disappointment are a part of maturity and growth.

For psychological health and well-being, you need clear boundaries and a real self, but this is not to say you don't need others. Interrelatedness is essential to being fully human. A healthy, real self makes it possible to experience true intimacy without loss of self and without overwhelming others with your dependency or neediness.

Experiences of true conversion ecstasy and communion with God are positive moments. But this is the coming together—the joining of real *persons*—as opposed to the vague merger of cosmic entities who dissolve into cosmic nothingness.

Psychologically speaking, the New Age movement does not herald a new and wondrous era for mankind. Rather it is an arrest in man's development. Morally, emotionally, and spiritually, it is infantile, pathological, and sinful.

On the surface, it sounds good. As a fallen human, I might even wish that the New Age view of things were correct. There is a certain appeal in believing that we are gods, that all our intentions are good, and that our potential is truly unlimited. But, alas, it is not true. Only by grace and maturity can we accept the horrible truth: We are limited mortals. Our hearts still share Adam and Eve's spirit of revolt, and the primal child in each of us still dreams of omnipotence. Lasch (1986, 16) said it well:

> The discovery that one's desires don't control the world—that human happiness is not the grand design underlying the creation of the universe—gives rise to a spirit of revolt. The idea that a benign creator could have made a world in which human happiness is not the overriding end offends human pride.

Which worldview we adopt has serious ramifications—psychological and otherwise—in all areas of our lives. Who we think man is—his limits, his potential, his destiny, crazy or blessed, god or mortal—is a matter of belief. How, and if, you help those who are hurt, disturbed, or in pain, is also determined by that belief.

9

THE FINAL THREAT: COSMIC CONSPIRACY AND END TIMES SPECULATION

SCP Staff

IT'S EASY TO BELIEVE IN CONSPIRACY.

Social experience teaches us that "inner rings" are real and numerous. Personal experience teaches us that sinister intentions, also real and numerous, are concealed as a matter of course. So it's logical to conclude that there may be inner rings that have made themselves totally invisible because their intentions are totally evil.

Logic aside, much of life lends itself to conspiracy thinking. As fallen beings in a fallen world, there is much we don't know. We not only fail to understand God, we don't even understand the evil we experience daily. Our existence in the world—in pain and vulnerability, transience and despair—presents us with a mystery. We face afflictions that are undeniably real, yet incomprehensible. The source of our miseries seems evasive and obscure, yet we cannot doubt that our miseries have a source. Thus we live in anxious ignorance and look for mysterious causes. *Voila*—it must be a conspiracy!

These tendencies are natural. The notion of conspiracy is psychologically plausible, and there is no intellectual default in thinking that conspiracies exist. The reason conspiracy theories often lack credibility is because they lack documentation. Of course, that's understandable, too. The most successful conspiracy is the one that is never discovered. So the lack of documentation does not deter those who hatch conspiracy theories. If anything, it has egged them on. When data is scanty, rumor and speculation fill the gaps. When the evidence is largely circumstantial, the net of circumstances can be extended as widely as the reach of mind will carry it. The concept of conspiracy becomes a screen on which a considerable range of theories can be projected.

Conspiracy theories have a long and fascinating history. One of the few unifying factors is the concept of "world conspiracy for world government."

In their book, *The Todd Phenomenon* (1979, 17, 18) Hicks and Lewis say the various theories:

> . . . agree on one thing: Somebody is conspiring to rule the world. The conspiracy has been identified as communism, the Illuminati, Neo-Nazism, the Mafia, the Rothschilds, international bankers, the Masons, the Catholic Church. . . . the Council on Foreign Relations, the Rockefellers, the Tri-Lateral Commission, occultism, Zionism, the Bildebergers, satanism, etc., etc. Some take the position that all of these are interconnected, highly organized and controlled by one mastermind, a political genius. When speaking

of the conspiracy, it is good to know which conspiracy theory one is talking about.

Extravagant allegations are the common fare of conspiracy fans. As a result, the very concept of a conspiracy vast enough to influence world events has been rejected and derided by academic historians. Serious belief in such machinations has been a distinctly minority hobby—until recently.

In the last twenty years, popular fascination with conspiracy theories has expanded enormously, and even the scholarly study of conspiracies has gained a tenuous enclave of respect. This has been the result of three dramatic developments.

1. The assassination of the Kennedys, Martin Luther King, Jr., and Malcolm X stirred up immediate and continuing conspiracy charges. Those killings put the suggestion of conspiracy into the public mind in a striking and credible way.
2. Watergate, the most exhaustively exposed conspiracy of our time, convinced us that it could happen here. Watergate revealed how easily the casual abuse of power is transformed into a real plot, and how readily it spreads, under the cover of rectitude and bland denial.
3. The emergence of international terrorism showed us how vulnerable the structures of power are to disruption by a few. The global network of interest and influence that we call international politics is so delicately balanced that any band of dedicated zealots can unsettle it. The idea of a worldwide plot no longer seems unfeasible or farfetched. The most disturbing lesson of all is that operations planned in secret and executed by surprise are almost impossible to stop.

Conspiracies are real, and they have real power—that is the latent message of today's news. Seldom before in history have so many people had so many rational reasons for believing in a superconspiracy. Popular entertainment has kept conspiracy consciousness at a high level by using the theme as a common plot device.

With a receptive audience at hand, it is no surprise that seasoned conspiracy theorists have stepped forward in droves to offer their own versions of the plot behind the turmoil of our times.

As these ideas emerged into general view, they have mingled with another minority interpretation of history: that of the fundamentalist and evangelical Christian. In particular, the most sensational themes of biblical prophecy—the last days, the Antichrist, the whore of Babylon, and the second coming of Christ—strikingly overlap the traditional conspiracy theory of a plot for global rule. Such a combination is not entirely unprecedented, but it has never found such an eager market or exercised so wide an influence. It has produced a unique genre of literature that could be called "Conspiracy Apocalyptic."

As various authors interpret the economic, political, and religious signs of the times, their books describe a conspiracy to engineer the imminent arrival of the Antichrist's demonic dictatorship. Depending on one's point of view, these publications have either alerted or alarmed a significant portion of the Christian public.

How should such cosmic-conspiracy theories be viewed? Are they perceptive or paranoid? Are they reliable guides to the future, or fanciful projections? Do they aid our understanding, or merely distract our attention? In order to answer such questions, the "Conspiracy Apocalyptic" scenario must be unraveled. We will briefly look at each of its components—the worldly and the Christian—in turn.

The Worldly Contribution

The worldly contribution provides the major outlines of the plot for global rule. According to the theory, men of wealth and power are cooperating worldwide, to overturn the established order and replace it with a new international regime of their own devising and control. A currently popular variation on this theme (Hunt 1983, 47) describes

> ... a conspiracy among top political leaders in Washington to betray America's national interests. These men, all members or former members of the Trilateral Commission and/or Council on Foreign Relations (CFR), are said to be working hand in glove with certain highly placed communist leaders in an international conspiracy to bring about a world government. Stretching from Washington to London, Paris, Bonn, Moscow and Tokyo, this mysterious web of intrigue is alleged to include the wealthiest families in the world. Names like Krupp, Rothschild and Rockefeller are mentioned along with the allegation that international bankers financed the Russian revolution 65 years ago and have been backing both sides in every war since then.

This is the basic no-frills conspiracy model. The normal instruments of rule are considered to be the objects of the plot. The normal human lust for power and gain is considered sufficient motive to account for the enterprise.

Expanded versions offer options that include high-powered ethnic, racial, and religious themes. A fundamental conflict between nationalism and internationalism is implicit in the worldview of all conspiracy theories. Because of their transnational identity, the Jews are a favorite target of conspiratoid accusations. So are the Catholic Church, the Masons, the international bankers—anyone with power and interests that extend beyond national political control. By status and by definition, their motives are suspect, their aims deemed subversive, and their methods assumed to be devious.

The occult variation. One influential conspiracy theory says that a secret occult organization has for many years been holding the destiny of empires hostage to its inscrutable will. This malign cult, the Illuminati (the illuminated, or enlightened ones), is said to be a secret society of powerful adepts who are striving to realize their ambition of global autocracy.

The modern Order of the Illuminati was founded in 1776 by Adam Weishaupt, a Bavarian professor of canon law at Ingolstadt University. The order offered eight stages of initiation toward illumination. It was radically humanistic ("Man is God") and radically subversive ("Away with all established monarchial and ecclesiastical authorities"). The anarchist activism of the order was uncovered by accident (or providence) when an Illuminati courier was struck and killed by lightning. His secret papers soon came to the attention of authorities, and the alarmed Bavarian elector had the order suppressed in 1785.

By that time, however, the virus of "illuminism" (according to the theory) had spread throughout Europe by infecting the lodges of Freemasonry. The pressure of official hostility in Bavaria simply hastened the diffusion of Illuminati ideas and influence. By 1789, it is claimed Weishaupt and his Illuminati network were potent enough to engineer the French Revolution, with its attack on traditional rule and its godless barbarities, in the name of reason, science, and humanism.

The political theory of evil. At this point, you can see how easily conspiracy theories get mixed up in politics. That is one reason why establishment historians seldom take conspiracy theories seriously. They look suspiciously like propaganda devices concocted to discredit the opposition.

Of course, a theory formulated by a partisan axe-grinder could still be true. Those who look for the worst may well find it, if it is there—or even if it is not. This is the baffling ambiguity of the conspiracy game. It makes the real truth about conspiracy theories almost impossible to discover.

The truth of most theories is inherently obscure and mostly irrelevant. What seems to be more important is their political base. Politics is always a major ingredient of any conspiracy theory, and in the end, political causes, issues, and positions define what is considered good and evil.

From the outset, the Illuminati scenario has been tangled in political intrigue. The theory was first systematically articulated in London by the ex-Jesuit Abbe Barruel (1741–1820). Barruel, a polemicist against the French revolutionary regime, published his expose in 1797. The same year, the Scot John Robison published "Proofs of a Conspiracy against all the Religions and Governments of Europe, carried on in the Secret Meetings of the Free Masons, Illuminati and Reading Societies."

In America, Federalist pastors in New England preached sensational sermons against their southern, Democratic opponents, alleging an Illuminati infestation. Thomas Jefferson was even implicated by the theory. A generation later, the Illuminati plot resurfaced. This time, the villains were not Thomas Jefferson and the Democrats, but the Masons.

The theory has also been harnessed to religious prejudice against Catholics, Jews, and Mormons. It was used by both sides in the slavery conflict. The most recent revival of Illuminati mongering goes back to the 1950s, when the John Birch Society offered its own streamlined version of the theory.

Metaphysical politics. Outside the United States, the Illuminati theory (in various forms) has served different causes in a similar way. Two high points of European "conspiring" will help illustrate the nature of the worldly contribution. One is the anti-Semitic forgery entitled *The Protocols of the Learned Elders of Zion*, which had an identifiable occult source. The other is Nesta Webster's grand synthesis of conspiracy thinking entitled *World Revolution*, which had an ostensibly Christian basis.

The Protocols, as the document has come to be known, is one of the most notorious frauds of history. It is also closely connected with the early history of Theosophy. Theosophists may have had a hand in writing *The Protocols*, and were demonstrably responsible for the forgery's distribution.

The Protocols purport to be the minutes of a meeting of conspirators discussing a plan to gain world control. The plot is masterminded by an international syndicate of Jews, who operate through the Freemasons and other secret societies (Webb 1976, 213–214):

So ruthless are the elders that they stop short of none of the repertoire of tricks normally reserved for mad scientists—the clandestine inoculation of diseases for example—and are even now burrowing beneath the earth, their sinister purposes camouflaged as the construction of underground railways, to create a network of tunnels from which they can blow up the capitals of Europe.

It has been shown that *The Protocols* were actually adapted from an 1864 satire on the authoritarian regime of France's Napoleon the Third. The forgery was composed in France during the late 1890s, at the height of France's anti-Semitic flap and occultic revival.

The document traveled from the French occult underground to Czarist Russia, where it found eager acceptance in the bizarre spiritual atmosphere of prerevolutionary Russia. *The Protocols* were issued in a variety of versions, many with extended commentary attached to explain the relevance of the document to the writer's own mystical or ideological hobbyhorse. One such version was published by the Orthodox cleric and mystic Sergio Nilus.

Nilus connected his manuscript of *The Protocols* with the expectation of the coming of the Antichrist which . . . was quite common in the Russian religious revival of the time. . . . He concocted a symbolic system that enabled him to detect the mark of Antichrist in almost any geometric design—including commercial trademarks.

Conspiracy theories do not stand alone. The biases of the theorists influence the conclusions, though most people who swallow the theories are not aware of the biases behind them. Thus, conspiracy theories may carry implications that are invisible but influential. The theories are often part of a package deal, so to speak.

192

Three kinds of biases are most often seen in world-conspiracy theories:

1. Extremist politics, usually of the right-wing variety
2. Involvement or fascination with occultism or esoteric spirituality
3. Religious prejudice, usually anti-Semitic or anti-Christian in nature.

The complete development of this syndrome is well illustrated in the person of Nesta H. Webster, author of *World Revolution* and one of the most influential conspiracy writers of our century.

Webster saw five powers supporting a world conspiracy: Grand Orient Masonry, Theosophy, pan-Germanism, international finance, and social revolution. Her work supplies the great part of the occult lore used in modern English and American conspiracy theories, most of which also follow the broad pattern of her portrayal.

Nesta Webster found her vocation in the exotic psychological borderlands between mysticism and activism. The implicit anti-Semitism of her thesis, with its emphasis on Jewish occultism as the key expression of demonic wisdom, eventually politicized her life. In the mid-1920s, she became a member of the British Fascisti, Great Britain's first Fascist movement. Webster thought of herself as a proponent of Christianity and a defender of Christian civilization against a vast and godless intrigue.

The Christian Contribution

The Christian community's interest in the end times, even if occasionally excessive, does not usually lead to conspiracy hunting. Most expositors of end-time prophecy have dealt with the themes of Antichrist, Babylon, apostasy, and so forth without raising the issue of a universal conspiracy.

One element of the biblical worldview, however, does create

an opening for conspiracy. Marsden (1980, 211) points out that fundamentalists are disposed

> . . . to divide all reality into neat antitheses: the saved and the lost, the holy and the unsanctified, the true and the false. Moreover their common sense philosophical assumption added the assurance that they could clearly distinguish these contrasting factors when they appeared in everyday life.

The biblical concepts of good, evil, and spiritual conflict are uncomplicated because they are basic. Evil, like good, is revealed by the Bible to be a unified system of influence, and there is a spiritual warfare being waged between God and Satan. But when we try to literally apply the revealed model of spiritual warfare to human society, we are headed for trouble. The spiritual sources of the conflict may be simple, but their historical expression is convoluted beyond comprehension. That is why terms like the "mystery of iniquity" and "mystery of godliness" are used in Scripture.

In a sense, then, when we impose the stark simplicity of spiritual conflict on the ambiguous complexity of the world, we explain away the mysteries. Whenever we try to connect all the dots to define "the mystery of evil," we inevitably inject our own bias into the drawing.

The New Age plot. The "Conspiracy Apocalyptic" genre plays heavily on the end-times unity of evil. According to it, there is a human superconspiracy going on right now, which is manipulating the world toward the final evil portrayed in the Book of Revelation. Several current best-sellers identify the New Age movement as a network of organizations and individuals consciously working to organize the world for the advent of a charismatic religious/political ruler—the Antichrist.

Perhaps the best-known book in this area is Constance Cumbey's *The Hidden Dangers of the Rainbow*. Cumbey's thesis is well summed up by a review in *Cornerstone* magazine (Pement 1983, 18):

The conspiracy is a network of all the cults, political and humanitarian organizations, and of isolated groups. The movement's directives are literally called "the Plan," articulated by Alice Bailey in the 1930s; now, they come from Lucis Trust in New York (custodian of Bailey's writings). The conspiracy follows Alice "like a recipe." The Antichrist who is to come is Lord Maitreya, a deity of Eastern and occultic lore, whom Cumbey believes is now incarnate (via demon possession).

When he is announced, all the world will have to undergo a Luciferic initiation and receive his mark. The vehicle which is coordinating the efforts to build the one-world government is Planetary Citizens (a New York-based corporation dedicated to creating a new global society), which, Cumbey says, "has established a timetable for taking over the world by summer solstice, or June 21, 1983."

On the positive side, Cumbey has effectively drawn attention to a phenomenon that deserves attention. The New Age movement exists, and its implications are serious. In addition, her picture of the movement's organizational network appears to be accurate and well documented. In this respect, her work is "performing a real service by raising the issue so loudly that it must be heard" (Marsden 1982, 9). The New Age movement is undoubtedly part of a gathering social and cultural transformation that is increasingly coherent and increasingly hostile to Christianity. It is well past time that Christians woke up to that fact.

Enter the Conspiratoids. The conspiracy theme, however, is disturbingly explicit in Cumbey's book. In a telephone interview, the author was asked if the New Age movement was a conspiracy involving thousands of persons, all plotting to take over the world for the same person, intelligently acting in concert.

Her reply was, "It is absolutely that!"

Elements of Cumbey's thesis have been taken from the worldly tradition of Illuminati-style theorizing. Her conspiracy scenario also depends heavily on two spiritually questionable sources, which claim to describe the conspiracy: Alice Bailey (occult) and Marilyn Ferguson (New Age). While both of these should be taken seriously, they need not be taken literally. Cumbey ignores the tendency of occult and New Age propagandists to weave conspiracy legends about themselves. She accepts their inflated self-images at face value and absorbs some of their unsavory spiritual implications, as well. Saying Alice Bailey's plan is truly the blueprint for our future amounts to saying that demonic revelation can flesh out our understanding of divine revelation. That is giving the devil more than his due.

The evidence of Cumbey's conspiracy is mostly circumstantial, and hence, members of the conspiracy are commonly identified by the causes they espouse and the positions they express. Thus a political standard comes to dominate the definition of the conspiracy. The worst of it is, as George Marsden (1982) says, "There is nothing quite like politics to divide Bible-believing Christians."

True to form, Cumbey's thesis turns its accusatory edge inward. Conflicts along political lines become the basis of division within the Church. Cumbey (1983) delivers several pages of accusation against identified evangelical writers. One of her chief targets is Tom Sine, author of *The Mustard Seed Conspiracy*. Her leading sentence of critique clearly sets the theme: "Perhaps it is coincidental that *Mustard Seed* contains some of the same programs as the New Age Movement." Stanley Mooneyham and World Vision come under fire in identical terms: "Mooneyham has long enjoyed great prominence in the Christian world. Yet his book, *What Do You Say to a Hungry World?* advocates much of the political program of the New Agers." Cumbey positions other Christian thinkers in the New Age camp because they use certain buzz words that are popular with New Age writers.

"The first thing noticeable about [this] book to one versed in New Age lore is [the author's] use of a vocabulary prevalent among New Agers. Words such as Spaceship Earth, vanguard, holistic, New Age, and global village are a common part of his vocabulary."

Cumbey's political emphasis is popular with her readers, who may even magnify the political conclusions in the future. If this happens, the consequences will, indeed, be unpleasant for evangelicals.

Certainly Christian leaders are not above criticism. If someone's thinking has been unduly influenced by the world's agendas and expectations, there is a place for saying so. However, there is no place for equating the use of popular clichés with participation in apocalyptic evil.

Theorizing and rationalizing. As we said earlier, the conspiracy model seeks to reduce a vast, discontinuous evil to a simple, identifiable course. But when conspiracies mix with apocalypse, conspiracy is sensationalized and apocalpyse is trivialized.

The reductionism of conspiracy ideas affects Cumbey's book in several ways. One of the most glaring is an attempt to technologize the supernatural. She asserts that the deceiving miracles of the false prophet (Revelation 13:13–15) will be faked by means of satellite-projected, laser-generated holographic images. Thus, the miraculous—that which exceeds human comprehension—is reduced to the level of human planning and capability.

History is reduced, as well. Only the influences that fit into the conspiracy model are considered significant.

The weakness of this approach is evident when Cumbey attempts to entangle evangelicals in her New Age net. The only reason she can think of for some Christians using New Age buzz words like *vanguard* or *global village* is the influence of the Lucis Trust. The only way to include that kind of influence in the plot is to opt for a cosmic cabal.

Cumbey does not go that far. Nor does her conspiracy vision explain our current situation. Today we are in the midst of a cultural/spiritual upheaval of almost inconceivable proportions. This cultural shift, like the Renaissance, is a shift in the general worldview, among other things. Its whole effect is to alter the terms by which people describe and understand reality. By definition, this means that people begin to think alike and to interpret problems in similar terms. Much of what is happening today is the result of multiple developments in diverse fields over several centuries. The conspiracy thesis accommodates none of these considerations.

The fact that Christians use language that New Agers use or advocate programs New Agers promote may be the effect of the shift that the non-Christian world is experiencing. The problem of New Age thinking in evangelical circles might be a problem of worldliness or of discernment, but it is not a problem of conspiracy.

Prophecy rationalized. The conspiracy assumption especially tends to rationalize biblical prophecy. It brings the ultimate confrontation of Scripture down to the very human scale of organizations, agents, and programs. It demands that prophecy give us detailed particulars on the political structure of the Antichrist's regime. It sees the Book of Revelation as a documentary of end-times events, and deciphers its symbolism accordingly. It uses Scripture as a picture of predictive detail, rather than a standard of discernment. At its base is a misunderstanding of apocalyptic prophecy and a misapplication of apocalyptic imagery.

If we use the Book of Revelation merely to look for the content of the future, we are beginning at the wrong end. John's apocalypse has much to say about specific events, and it predicts them in some detail. Nevertheless, its descriptions must be interpreted and applied in the light of the book's basic message. The Book of Revelation is less revealing about the details of history than it is about the nature of history. It tells us that:

1. History is governed by God. His purposes are secure, despite the turmoil and confusion of conflict. God not only triumphs over history, but *in* history.
2. History has a climax. It has an end. It is not eternal or cosmically repetitive.
3. The end of history will be characterized by a final intensification of the fundamental conflict that pervades all of history. Conflict will be with us until the end of history, because in a fallen world, history *is* conflict, and conflict *is* history.

The apostle John depicts this final conflict in vivid and compelling imagery. The character of God's adversary is fully exposed, as Satan rouses himself for his ultimate confrontation with his enemy and judge. In Revelation, we have a picture of evil utterly unrestrained in its intentions, with its lying, murderous nature on full display.

This is a prophecy of the future, and it is clear that at some point this evil will manifest itself concretely in history, in a form as pure as that which John foresaw. It is also a commentary on the present: The spirit of Antichrist is always with us; its diluted influence can be discerned in many a tinhorn dictator and two-bit messiah.

At times, however, the Antichrist spirit is stronger than at others. John's day was such a time; our own day is another. In times like these, the structure and dynamics of human society will more and more resemble the pure form of evil depicted in the apocalypse. In John's time, this trend was eventually reversed. In our time, the issue is yet to be resolved.

In any case, the prophecy gives us a scale of comparison by which we can evaluate any historical period, including our own. It will give us discernment of current events, but it will not give us the details of their development. The events surrounding the emergence of the Antichrist (for example, the numbering system, the false miracles, the apostate church, and so on) are part of a universal pattern, revealed in its final configuration. The prophet does not give us the historical particulars so much as a look at what determines the particulars. He does not describe the details of the end-time events so much as he describes their dynamics—a much more valuable revelation.

If we insist on looking for a blueprint of expectation in prophecy, if we try to decode it as concrete detail, we will miss the point. We will make Scripture into a device for divination, instead of a tool of discernment. We will end up with a reductionistic scenario that is distorted by rationalism, tainted with speculation, oriented to politics, and marginally useful if accurate, which is highly unlikely.

Summary and Conclusion

Conspiracy theories are believable, but not verifiable. This creates a space for the free play of anxiety and speculation. As a result, the conspiracy-theory tradition has incorporated many elements that are suspect in their origins and disruptive in their effects.

The conspiracy tradition is intriguing and suggestive. Sometimes it may even contain an element of truth. But it is a tainted stream. It will not aid our Christian understanding. The genre contains too many false trails and psychospiritual booby traps, to be useful. If it is employed at all, it will almost certainly import some alien and adulterating qualities into biblical analysis. "Conspiracy Apocalyptic" literature illegitimately mixes theological concepts with rationalistic speculations about human affairs.

The ultimate tendency of the conspiracy concept is reductionistic. It will limit our understanding of Scripture, producing a picture that humanizes the "mystery of iniquity" and distracts our understanding from the real focus of the biblical prophecies. As a result, the issues are politicized, and the net effect is to divide Christians against one another on the basis of an essentially political standard of judgment.

Scripture casts the definitive light on conspiracy theorizing:

The problem is as old as Eden. The Fall itself was a serpentine plot—the serpent enlisted a naive Eve on behalf of his hidden agenda. Conspiracy theories soon ensued: The first were Adam's and Eve's explanations of their bungle (*see* Genesis 3:9–13).

That pattern of primal tragedy tells us three important things:

1. There really is a conspiracy;
2. Theories about it generally begin in fear and end in rationalization;
3. The theories tend to be diversions, even when factually accurate.

Wisdom is not served by reducing Satan's purposes to a plot of local yokels. When the Bible speaks of conspiracy theories specifically, it ignores the issue of accuracy altogether. It simply directs our attention to God—which is where it truly belongs.

> For thus the Lord spoke to me with mighty power and instructed me not to walk in the way of his people, saying, "You are not to say, 'It is a conspiracy!' in regard to all that this people call a conspiracy. And you are not to fear what they fear or be in dread of it. It is the Lord of hosts whom you should regard as holy. And he shall be your fear. And He shall be your dread" (Isaiah 8:11–13 NAS).

PART FOUR

REAPING THE HARVEST— ANTIDOTE

10

SPIRITUAL AUTISM: BREAKING BARRIERS BY BUILDING BRIDGES

Dean C. Halverson

RAUN WAS EIGHTEEN MONTHS OLD AND AUTISTIC. EVERY DAY, HE withdrew into his self-enclosed world. He didn't acknowledge the presence of his own family, he didn't talk, and he seemed to be deaf. Most of the day, he sat on the floor and rocked, oblivious to his surroundings.

Raun's parents loved him too much to give up on him by institutionalizing him. Since he wouldn't join them in their world, they determined to join him in his. First they observed and catalogued his actions, then they imitated him—rocking, spinning, and flapping. With the help of friends, they committed twelve hours a day, seven days a week, to their son. As a result of their love and efforts to reach him, Raun was transformed into a communicative, playful, loving, and outgoing child within a year.

Basically, we are all spiritually autistic: We prefer to depend on ourselves, rather than God. Just as Raun closed himself off from his parents, so we close ourselves off from God. The New Age movement, however, raises spiritual autism to a new level.

Not only have New Agers closed themselves off from God, they have elevated themselves to the level of gods, claiming to be cocreators of the universe. In *The Aquarian Conspiracy* (1980), Marilyn Ferguson says our brains construct hard reality. Michael Talbot (1981) refers to human beings as reality-structurers. While promoting humanity to the level of gods, they have demoted God to the level of an impersonal oneness, a manipulable inner force. This "god" is seen as being the source for humanity's self-empowerment. Such is the nature of spiritual autism.

Many Christians are asking how to break through this spiritually autistic system and reach the New Ager with the Gospel of Jesus Christ. The only way his parents could help Raun become aware of external relationships was through their incarnational love, as they joined him in his world. That is the way God personally broke into the history of humanity in the person of Jesus Christ. And that is the way we must break through to New Agers today. Our evangelistic approach must be incarnational.

The Need to Communicate

The first thing Raun's parents did to reach him was observe his behavior carefully. After they became familiar with it, they copied his every action. If he rocked, they rocked; if he pounded, they pounded.

Such an approach may remind you of Paul's primary principle of evangelism: "Though I am free and belong to no man, I make myself a slave to everyone, to win as many as possible. . . .

I have become all things to all men so that by all possible means I might save some" (1 Corinthians 9:19, 22). Paul became all things to all men because he wanted to *communicate* the Gospel, not merely proclaim it. He wanted to produce changed lives, not merely pass on an intellectual understanding of the Gospel.

When he tried to evangelize the philosophers of Athens, he did his homework by first studying their culture. Luke wrote: "Paul then stood up in the meeting of the Areopagus and said: 'Men of Athens! I see that in every way you are very religious. For as I walked around and looked carefully at your objects of worship, I even found an altar with this inscription: TO AN UNKNOWN GOD'" (Acts 17:22, 23). The term translated "see" is *thereo*, a word that signifies looking at something with interest and for a purpose. The word connotes the picture of a physician examining a patient and looking for the cause of an illness.

Evangelism is more than haphazardly sowing the seed of the Gospel: It is translating the message of Jesus into the language of the hearer. If you can empathize with another's view of reality, then you will be able to address the needs they feel are important. When you can speak to them from their own frame of reference, it is more likely they will listen and heed your words.

Jim Petersen (1982, 41), formerly a missionary to Brazil, gives good advice when he says that evangelists must "close the gap successfully between themselves as communicators and the members of their audience. This requires two things: an understanding of the hearer's thought patterns, and the translation of the gospel message into their everyday language."

When the apostle John used the Greek term *logos* in his Gospel, he was translating the Gospel message into the language of his readers. *Logos* originally referred to the all-pervading organizing principle within all things. John emptied the term of its impersonal nature and gave it flesh and form in the person of Jesus Christ.

In a similar way, you could translate certain concepts of the New Age movement.

Consider, for example, their belief that by our observation, we "actualize" (organize) the chaos of reality. According to New Agers, the act of observation brings one of the infinite possibilities into actuality. When Gary Zukav (1979, 102) rhetorically asked: "How is the universe being actualized?" he replied: "The answer comes full circle. We are actualizing the universe."

Although New Agers claim that the new physics supports their worldview, they really cut the legs from under science by denying that there is anything out there at all. In addition, they cannot adequately explain why the realities that you may actualize correspond at all with the realities that I actualize. The only adequate explanation for such correspondence is in the transcendent God, who *does* actualize the universe. Jesus Christ is the actualizer of all things (John 1:3; Colossians 1:16, 17). The answer to the question, "How is the universe being actualized?" does not come full circle and end in us, but in God and His Son, Jesus Christ.

Another way to close the gap between New Agers and ourselves is to look for the signs of Himself that God has left in their worldview. Paul built his Areopagus address (Acts 17:22–31) around such signs. For example, he used the altar to an unknown god to point out the Athenian's acknowledgment of their ignorance of God. He also referred to two Greek poets who spoke of the nearness of God and of the fact that we are His offspring.

God has also left signs of Himself in the New Age movement. For example, the spiritual change required in a person is often described by New Agers as an "awakening." The theme of spiritual awakening is, indeed, a high New Age priority. The following quote by Georges Gurdjieff, a Greek-Armenian mystic philosopher and teacher, appeared in a promotional brochure for a New Age conference. It captures some essentials of the New Age perspective, which could be used in evangelism. The quote mentions such themes as our condition of being spiritually asleep, the urgency of the need to be awakened, and the fact that we cannot awaken ourselves:

A man is immersed in dreams. . . . Then he wakes up. At first glance this is a quite different state of consciousness. He can move, he can talk with other people. . . . But if we go a little more deeply into things, we shall see that he is in almost the same state as when he is asleep. And it is even worse, because in sleep he is passive. In the waking state he can do something all the time. . . .

Let us take some event in the life of humanity. For instance, war. There is a war going on at the present moment. What does it signify? It signifies that several millions of sleeping people are trying to destroy several millions of other sleeping people. They would not do this, of course, if they were to wake up. Everything that takes place is owing to this sleep. . . .

How many times have I been asked here whether wars can be stopped? Certainly they can. . . . It is only necessary that people should awaken. It seems a small thing. It is, however, the most difficult thing there can be because this sleep is induced and maintained by the whole of surrounding life. . . .

How can one awaken? How can one escape this sleep? These questions are the most important, the most vital that can ever confront a man. . . .

A man cannot awaken *by himself*. . . . People must be looked after by a man who is not asleep or who does not fall asleep as easily as they do. . . . They must find such a man *and hire him* to wake them and not allow them to fall asleep again. Without this it is impossible to awaken. This . . . must be understood.

That is indeed a strong statement of our need for spiritual awakening or regeneration.

New Agers repeatedly admit that something is wrong with humanity and the individual must be transformed before we can have global harmony. Ferguson (1980, 28, italics mine)

209

writes that we must see "that the escalating crisis is a symptom of our *essential wrongheadedness*." Similarly, Rajneesh (1984, B2) has written: "My message to humanity is a new man. Less than that won't do. Not something modified, not something continuous with the past, but utterly discontinuous. Something very basic has gone wrong."

We can draw upon such New Age statements to communicate to New Agers that something is, indeed, wrong with humanity. But the problem goes deeper than they imagine. It goes beyond merely a change in consciousness or an adoption of a new worldview. Christian transformation extends to our basic nature. We have within us a spirit of death: God wants to give us the Spirit of life.

Redemptive analogies can also be found in the area of the New Age movement's concept of God. New Agers teach that God is an impersonal organizing force that is mystically immanent in all things and, in fact, *is* all things. The vital issue for evangelism has to do with God's personhood. Even though New Agers explicitly deny God's personhood, they still imply it in their language and their worldview.

For example, although Ferguson rejects the personhood of God, she describes God as being "the consciousness that manifests as lila," "the organizing matrix we can experience but not tell," and "that which enlivens matter" (1980, 382). Attributes such as consciousness, rationality, and the ability to create or enliven are personal attributes, not impersonal. Although such attributes exist to lesser degrees in other forms of life, there is nothing more aware, more rational, and more full of life than a person.

As couriers of God's message, we must learn to build bridges to, rather than barriers against, New Agers. Often Christians believe they must demolish the opposing worldview before they can convince the person of the truth of Christianity. Such a view confuses the distinction between being a defender of the faith and a Christian apologist. As an evangelist, Paul was an apologist, not a defender. He found as much common ground as possible with those he wanted to reach, even while he challenged their position (Green 1970, 128).

One theologian elaborated on the difference between being an apologist and a defender of the faith like this (Chadwick 1955, 275):

> Paul's genius as an apologist is his astonishing ability to reduce to an apparent vanishing point the gulf between himself and his converts and yet to "gain" them for the Christian gospel. . . . The apologist must minimize the gap between himself and his potential converts. Very different is the psychological attitude of the defender of orthodoxy; he must make as wide as possible the distance between authentic Christianity and deviationist sects against whose teaching the door must be closed with all firmness.

While I am in no way suggesting we compromise either the Gospel of Jesus Christ or the uniqueness of God's revealed Word, nevertheless, God has left signs in other belief systems that we can use to point others to Him.

The Need for Relevance

New Agers talk a great deal about the need for personal transformation and personal affirmation. These are phrases that Christians also relate to, and they provide an opening for Christian witnessing.

Personal transformation. Every religion says that some defect exists within humanity and that this defect will be remedied when a spiritual connection is made with the divine. The New Age movement is no exception. Physicist Fritjof Capra (1982) suggests that for transformation to take place, we need a new view of reality, where the concept of the human spirit is understood "as the mode of consciousness in which the individual feels connected to the cosmos as a whole."

Such an experience of cosmic interconnectedness has moral consequences, according to New Agers. It is the catalyst for a new humanity, a humanity with the power to live in harmony. Peter Russell, in *The Global Brain,* (1983) says, "A genuine love for the rest of creation comes from the personal experience of oneness with the rest of creation, the awareness that, at the deepest level, the Self and the world are one." Similarly, Ferguson believes that such an experience of interconnectedness compels one toward brotherhood:

"When the self joins the Self, there is power. Brotherhood overtakes the individual like an army . . . not the obligatory ties of family, nation, church, but . . . a spiritual fusion. This discovery transforms strangers into kindred, and we know a new, friendly universe."

One way to describe the defect within humanity is to say we are alienated from one another and from God. New Agers solve the problem by denying the otherness of anything. If you say that everything is one, how can there be any alienation?

But how does this "spiritual fusion" take place?

One New Age statement reads: "The transformation we seek is personal as well as global: it must begin with us. . . . Our aim is to empower ourselves and others for personal and global transformation." A New Age radio station opens with the words: "It is only through a change of consciousness that the world will be transformed. As we bring mind, body, psyche and spirit into harmony and unity, so also will the world be changed. This is our responsibility, as we create and explore New Dimensions of being."

Although New Agers admit that humanity is in some way defective, nevertheless, they maintain the solution resides in ourselves.

The problem is that New Agers confuse self-empowerment with personal transformation. The two are actually mutually exclusive. Self-empowerment trusts in our own inner power; personal transformation trusts in the power of the holy God. Self-empowerment glorifies the self; personal transformation glorifies God. Self-empowerment merely adds power to man's fallen nature. With personal transformation, however, God adds life to a nature that was bent toward death.

By its very nature, spiritual autism withdraws into itself and refuses to acknowledge the necessity for an external relationship with God. But such an external relationship is the only source of hope, if a transformation is ever to occur. Just as Raun could not transform himself by means of his own power, neither are we adequate to change ourselves. Transformation can come only from outside ourselves—from a personal God.

Personal affirmation. *Total* self-acceptance is the name of the game in the New Age movement. One main tenet of Lifespring, a human-potential group, is this (Hanley, nd, 3): "We are perfect exactly the way we are. And when we accept that, life works." Such a statement is typical of the New Age movement. The concept of total self-acceptance strikes a positive chord within us. We want to feel good about ourselves. We need to know we are valuable as persons.

But there is a catch. Although New Agers assert the value of the individual on the psychological level, their belief system denies it on the ultimate, spiritual level. The goal of the spiritual journey on which Rajneesh sends his followers is for the individual to disappear into the oneness of God (1977, 100; 1975, 23):

> The enlightenment happens only when the ego has disappeared. The ego is the darkness of the soul, the ego is the imprisonment of the soul, the "I" is the barrier to the ultimate . . . *You* will never encounter God. If *you* are there, God is not there because the seed [ego] is there. When you disappear, God is there; so there is no encounter really.

If ultimate reality is, indeed, impersonal, then the individual is worthless. Impersonality obliterates the value of personality. New Agers may assert a kind of affirmation of the personal, but their words are empty without a personal God as the foundation for reality (Schaeffer 1972).

213

In an evangelistic encounter between Vishal Mangalwadi (a Christian who, with his wife, directs the Theological Research and Communications Institute in New Delhi) and a Hindu, Vishal explained the inevitable conclusion of the monistic view that ultimate reality is impersonal (Mangalwadi 1984, 18–19):

> *Vishal:* Is . . . Universal Consciousness personal or impersonal?
> *Hindu:* It is impersonal and infinite.
> *V:* Is personality higher than impersonality?
> *H:* Of course!
> *V:* Then why do you want to become lower and merge into impersonal consciousness?
> *H:* Well, no. Personality is actually lower than impersonality.
> *V:* Why do you then use the term evolution? You should say we have devolved out of the impersonal. Then you should really respect this grass on which we are sitting. Being impersonal, it is higher than us, and you should not walk on it.
> *H:* This is confusing.

Yes, it is confusing, and that's because the lives and beliefs of New Agers do not mesh. Their actions show that they find meaning and value in relating to others, but according to their teachings, there is no value in a personal relationship with God. Instead, they want to lose themselves in an impersonal oneness.

Of course, the idea of inner divinity is appealing. On the surface, it offers the ultimate in personal affirmation. But the problem is, when all of reality is divine, then you are no more valuable than a rock. We cannot live consistently with the implications of ultimate reality being impersonal, because it is in personal relationships that we naturally find value and fulfillment. How could this be any less true when talking about our relationship with God?

The Need for Confession

In announcing a new Lifespring course, its authors said they would teach the students that each of us is at cause in our lives. The idea of being "at cause"—or accountable for one's life—is a major theme in Lifespring. One Lifespring trainer represented the typical interpretation of being at cause when he said we are accountable for everything that happens to us—from the moment we pick our parents until we choose the moment of our death. That is total accountability. It assumes we have the potential power to control all things. Such is the nature of spiritual autism: It is self-sufficient, self-engaged, and self-adoring.

Just as those who work with the psychologically autistic try to help them become aware of external relationships, so those of us who work with the spiritually autistic should seek to help them become aware of their need for a relationship with God. The experience of guilt and confession can be useful here.

Most New Agers arrive at their self-oriented worldview through both intellectual investigation and experiential investigation. Through such techniques as biofeedback, meditation, self-hypnosis, guided imagery, and centering, they experience a certain power and control. When such experiences occur within the context of the New Age worldview, people interpret the experiences to mean they have been in touch with ultimate reality and have an unlimited amount of power within themselves.

Experientially based beliefs are not easily dislodged. Often they can be dislodged only by an experience as intense as the one that influenced them in the first place.

The release from guilt and the feeling of cleanness that follows confession is the type of experience that can help dislodge a New Ager's beliefs and point him in the direction of a sovereign, holy God. We are alienated from one another not because we are ignorant of our essential oneness, but because we are alienated from the person of God. Because of such alienation, we close ourselves off from God, depend on ourselves, and become self-oriented. In short, we become spiritually autistic. What is needed is reconciliation, and that comes through confession and forgiveness. God, through Jesus Christ, already offers the forgiveness and the possibility of reconciliation. We as Christians must encourage the New Ager to experience the great sense of release that comes from confessing such spiritual autism and claiming God's gift of forgiveness.

How can we convince New Agers of their guilt before a personal God and their need for confession to God? We can't.

Convicting people of sin is the work of the Holy Spirit, who "will convict the world of guilt in regard to sin and righteousness and judgment" (John 16:8). Since you can't do it, and only the Holy Spirit can work in a person's heart, prayer is essential. We are merely messengers: Jesus Christ is the message.

Although we cannot convict a person of sinfulness, we can help him become aware of the logical conclusion of his beliefs. For instance, New Agers say that objective reality is not brought into being until we observe it. The logical conclusion, of course, is that they must call themselves "creators." If they claim the power to manipulate ultimate reality, the very substance of God, then they should be able to affirm loudly—in fact, they should be able to shout—"I am god! I create reality! I am perfect!" If they can proclaim such statements without any hesitation or qualm, they probably will not be able to see their need to submit themselves to the Lordship of Christ. If, however, they hesitate and are struck by the pride required to claim such things, they may see their need for confession. It may provide an opening in the soil, where the seed of salvation can take root.

Before we use such an approach on a New Ager, however, we must first recognize that the problem is universal. There is the same inherent inclination in all of us to usurp the authority of God and trust in our own power. Once we understand how fallenness affects our lives, too, our evangelistic approach becomes much more empathetic and genuine. As we disclose our lives to others, we become vulnerable, and as we become vulnerable, they will see more easily the true source of Christian strength, peace and hope: Jesus Christ.

The Need for Answers

New Agers often have strong opinions about Christianity. They may feel that Christianity is pridefully exclusive, archaic, judgmental, powerless, divisive, or just plain irrelevant. Such preconceptions make it difficult for us to explain the biblical view of reality to New Agers.

Exclusivity and truth. Global unity is very dear to every New Ager. According to New Age teaching, one of the biggest problems in attaining global unity has been the divisiveness of religion. What we need to do, according to New Agers, is look beyond the surface differences and go to the essence of each religion. At that place, all religions are the same, they say. The way to God is like a large mountain, and just as there are many paths to the top, so there are many paths to God.

Former Astronaut Edgar Mitchell says (1983): "I have a feeling . . . that if we had Lao-tze, Buddha, Jesus, Mohammed, Moses, and Zoroaster all in the same room, they wouldn't have much disagreement of what was the relationship between man and divine reality."

So when Christians claim that Jesus Christ is the only way to God, New Agers vehemently object. One person wrote that such an attitude of exclusivism is motivated by "SPIRITUAL PRIDE, the worst sin. . . . You [Christians] feel sure that you have cornered the market on the truth."

All religions are not the same, however, even in their essence. Just look at their teachings. Hinduism is pantheistic, Buddhism is atheistic, many tribal religions are polytheistic, pagan religions are animistic, Christianity is theistic. Neither do all religions worship the same God. Judaism and Islam are strictly unitarian, whereas Christianity is trinitarian. Nor do the various religions agree on solutions to humanity's problems. Hare Krishnas say we are caught on the wheel of death and rebirth, and we can escape the wheel only by renouncing material pleasures and devoting ourselves and our thoughts to Krishna. Rajneesh says our basic problem is that we are ignorant of our divine nature. As a solution, he says we must detach ourselves from our separate egos and lose ourselves in the impersonal oneness of God. Christianity says we are by nature dead in our sins, and there is no hope in ourselves. Only by trusting in Jesus Christ can we have eternal life and come into a relationship with God. Religions are not only different; they are irreconcilable.

It is true that Jesus Christ does not claim to be merely a way shower or a way, but *the* Way (*see* John 14:6; Acts 4:12). Christianity is, by its very nature, exclusive.

The central issue, however, should not be that of exclusivity or inclusivity, narrow-mindedness or open-mindedness, bigotry or tolerance, but "What is truth?" Not all religions can be true, because their claims are mutually exclusive: God can ultimately be impersonal or personal, but not both.

Our lives depend upon our making distinctions. Every time we approach a stoplight, we distinguish between red and green. To say that we must be open-minded and accept the essential sameness of all colors could be fatal. In the same way, we must make distinctions between truth and falsehood in our everyday lives. We hear some ideas and judge them to be false; we hear others and accept them as true. All ideas cannot be accepted as true. If the New Agers' view of reality is true, then Christianity's view must be false. Both cannot be true.

How narrow is truth? Is there really only one path, as the Bible claims? If there is only one Way, how can God be called loving?

According to the Bible, the Way to God is narrow (Matthew 7:13, 14). It says originally there were two options: one that depended on humanity's efforts and one that depended on God's efforts. The Bible calls the first the way of the law, and the second the way of grace. In the way of the law, there is no mercy; only perfection will pass. Our sinful condition, however, makes law an impossible way to get to God. Inevitably that path leads us to death.

In the way of grace, however, we can find mercy. In God's Way, we can find forgiveness and reconciliation through the work of God's Son, Jesus Christ. God's solution to our problems is the only one that works. That solution is sufficient to pay for our sins, and it is also consistent with God's holy character. This is what the Bible means when it says that God is both "just and the one who justifies the man who has faith in Jesus" (Romans 3:26). The Way is narrow precisely because the gift of grace, like any gift, cannot be earned; it can only be received.

God's love vs. His justice. Another question that New Agers often raise is: How can a loving God condemn a person, a part of His own creation, to eternal damnation? It's a good question, and it requires an answer not only from the head, but also from the heart. In fact, when we look into God's Word for answers to this question, we discover that the Bible answers on the heart level as well as the head level.

The Bible declares that God is "patient with [us], not wanting anyone to perish, but everyone to come to repentance" (2 Peter 3:9). We were not meant for judgment from God, but for fellowship with Him.

So why does God judge? The core tension is not between God's love and His justice, but between God's will and our will. Because we have chosen to assert our will over His, we have alienated ourselves from God. God does not want to be eternally separated from us. The choice was ours. We have consistently rejected Him. God allows our desire for autonomy to result in eternal separation from Him. Eternal separation is the result of our will, not God's. Although God hounds us with His love, our prideful nature keeps us from admitting our weakness and depending on Him.

When New Agers object to God's right to judge, they are refusing to look at their own guilt. Here are some questions you can pose to New Agers: Are they as concerned about how well they live up to their own sense of love and justice as they are about how well God lives up to it? Do they themselves judge others for not meeting some standard? If they themselves judge others, are they not being hypocritical in saying that God doesn't have the right to judge?

God's infinity and His personhood. Another difficulty New Agers have with Christianity is understanding how God can be both personal and infinite. Personality is inherently limited, according to New Agers. They believe only an impersonal God, who is beyond all distinctions, could be infinite. But when New Agers say that God is beyond distinctions of good and evil, they are plunging into the realm of moral indefiniteness, not the realm of the infinite.

Infinity is more a quality than a quantity. To say God is infinite with respect to time means He is beyond time, not bound by time. To say God is infinitely good means He is perfect and whole in His goodness, and there is not even a hint of evil within Him. To say God is infinite in His presence means He is equally and wholly present to all things simultaneously. Properly understood, infinity can describe God alone, not His finite creation or some monistic god who is identified with creation.

To say God is beyond all distinctions is a meaningless statement that makes God a nothingness. Such a God is not infinite, but merely indefinite.

The real questions New Agers must deal with are: How can you place inherent value on personality, if God is impersonal? And where do you find meaning, if God is impersonal?

Reincarnation and biblical reliability. New Agers often charge that references to reincarnation were deleted from the original versions of the New Testament, and so our current versions of Scripture are unreliable. Such accusations do not stand up to the facts. Because of the massive amount of manuscript evidence, we are certain that the Bible, in its present form, accurately represents the original manuscripts.

New Agers also allege that the early Church believed in and taught reincarnation.

The fact is that reincarnation was never raised as an issue in any Church council during the first thousand years of the Church's existence. The only issue even remotely resembling reincarnation was Origen's belief in the preexistence of the soul. The issue of preexistence was discussed in the Council of Constantinople in AD 553, but it was condemned. Even though Origen believed in the preexistence of the soul, he denied the existence of reincarnation. The truth is that the early Church councils never considered reincarnation because reincarnation was bad news when compared to the good news of being resurrected to be with Jesus Christ.

Paradoxically, while New Agers use certain Bible passages to "prove" reincarnation, they also criticize Scripture for having been tampered with and for being unreliable. They can't have it both ways. If the Bible is unreliable, it cannot be called upon to support any position. If it is reliable, then it deserves to be examined without bias, as it stands.

The Need to Listen

Although it is often necessary for us to meet New Agers on an intellectual level, it is also important for us to meet them on a personal level. If we wish to move our conversation away from the abstract and into the personal realm, we might ask New Agers to tell us what their relationship has been to Christianity and what their understanding of Christianity is. Perhaps they would even be willing to give their testimony as to how they came to believe as they do. Later, we might wish to give our own testimony, but it is more effective to hear the other person's story first. There are at least two advantages to doing this. Listening to their testimony will put their objections or preconceptions in the context of their lives. We will gain insight about why they hold such ideas, who or what has influenced them, what they believe about God, how much they know about their belief system, and how strongly they hold it. Listening will also help us discern whether we are dealing with major or minor issues.

Before we take the time to deal with an issue, we must be sure it is a major obstacle to their coming to faith in Christ. Arguing about minor issues often accomplishes nothing but produces hard feelings and further entrenchment of the present belief system. Once we have come down to a major issue, we can ask questions, to be sure we understand their point of view. Ask them to express how they think the Bible or a typical Christian would answer their question. By listening carefully, we will be better able to give a thoughtful response. Evangelism really starts with understanding those to whom we are witnessing, and that kind of understanding only comes through listening.

Second, we not only receive a message when we listen, but we also convey one. The message we convey is our belief that they have personal worth, not only in our eyes, but also in the eyes of God. We may verbally tell a New Ager that he or she has personal worth, but our words seem empty if we never honor them enough to listen to what they say. New Agers often see Christians as narrow-minded and anxious to shove religion down a victim's throat, but if we sit down and listen, such a stereotype is dispelled. In its place may develop a more positive image of the Christian as one who cares.

The Need for Incarnational Love

God's most useful tool for evangelism is a life that is committed to Jesus Christ and willing to incarnate His love in the lives of others. This is the lesson we learn from the following story that tells of how one New Ager came to Jesus.

Beth had a problem of emotional insecurity that resulted in harbored resentment and an inability to forgive others. She tried individual and group therapy and many New Age workshops and techniques to overcome this problem, such as rebirthing, encounter groups, past-life regression, visualization, and affirmations. She was presently into *A Course in Miracles* by Gerald Jampolsky, which taught her to forgive others by changing her perceptions of them. After being hurt by one person, Beth remembers writing in her journal: "She is Love. She isn't really hurting me. I made a mistake when I chose hurt. She is love, just as I am." Beth said that this worked fine when she was by herself, but when she got involved in a close relationship again, she realized she didn't know anything about forgiveness.

She began to get involved with a man named Harry. Their relationship began with the understanding that they were perfect in their true selves and that they would accept each experience only as a lesson to be learned. After a while, they began to think about marriage. But as time went on, Beth saw that Harry was not living up to her standard of perfection. The culmination of Beth's disappointment came when Harry had another affair. When Harry told Beth, she was devastated. She had been taught through New Age counseling that if you love someone, allowing them to love others will only add to your relationship. But deep inside, she thought, "I don't care whether it's spiritually enlightened or not. I want someone who will be faithful in our relationship."

In an attempt to restore their relationship, Harry and Beth went to Puerto Rico, which is where they had previously planned to get married. While there, Harry looked up a friend named Sam who, to Harry's surprise, had become a minister.

As Beth came to know Sam, she was struck by his sincerity and eagerness to please the Lord, and by his willingness to serve others. She began to go to Sam for counseling. Unlike before—when she had paid $200–$500 for a weekend workshop or $60 an hour for a New Age counseling session—Sam was willing to spend time with her, even though he didn't know if she would see him again or put any money in the offering plate. She realized she had talked a lot about "unconditional love," but she was overwhelmed by Sam's actual demonstration of unconditional love.

After one particularly stormy counseling session where Beth blew up at Harry for his lack of commitment, Beth felt that Sam would never want to see her again. But the next day she saw only empathetic compassion on his face. She and Harry discovered, through Sam's wife, Anna, that for every hour he had spent in counseling with them, he had prayed two hours. Both Harry and Beth were so touched by Sam and Anna's love that they decided to take their advice to read the Bible and pray together. They found praying together did more for their relationship than all their New Age counseling put together.

During one sermon about God's gift of Jesus Christ, Beth began to think about her constant feeling that, "I am not enough." It seemed simple to change that thought to, "I am enough," but she wasn't able to do it. As the preacher preached, Beth began to realize that her "enoughness" was not the issue, at all. The issue was Jesus' "enoughness."

Later, while on the beach, the church sang, "I have decided to follow Jesus." Although Beth hadn't fully reconciled all the intellectual issues concerning Christianity, because of the love of Jesus that she had seen through Sam and Anna, she and Harry decided to follow Jesus. At that moment, she discovered both the forgiveness of God and the ability to forgive. "After placing my trust in the 'enoughness' of Jesus Christ," Beth said, "I am amazed at how completely my burden of guilt has been lifted."

The evangelistic value of a life that is committed to Jesus Christ and incarnates His love in the lives of other people should never be underestimated.

Conclusion

I saw a sign in a Berkeley store window that illustrates the chasm that separates the vision of the New Age movement from reality. The sign said: "We can make the world better—if we just do it." The first part of that statement represents the extreme optimism of the New Age movement, the vision of interpersonal and global harmony: We can make the world better. But that statement of extreme optimism is followed by a hint of doubt, a distant note of despair: If we just do it. Those last words linger in the mind. But *why* can't we seem to do it? The reality of disharmony stands in the face of the New Age vision of harmony.

New Agers tenaciously persist in their hope that we can change the world. And where is the focus of their hope? In humanity's unlimited potential and vision of oneness. In other words, the solution to humanity's problem is in ourselves. Such is the nature of spiritual autism; it is a spirituality caught up in itself.

The purpose of evangelism is to help the New Ager realize that inner potential and the vision of oneness is not enough to solve humanity's problems. They're not enough because humanity's core problem is not unrealized potential or blurred vision, but a broken relationship. At the very core of our being is a broken relationship caused by our spirit of self-centered pride and lawless rebellion against an absolutely holy God. The same self-centered pride that caused us to place ourselves above the law of God causes us to place our own interests over those of other people, other nations, and the land, as well.

We are the problem, not the solution. The solution to humanity's problems will be found only as we realize we need help from beyond ourselves, and that does not mean becoming mystically aware of some pantheistic, impersonal god who represents our unlimited potential. Instead, it means the restoration of a relationship that we purposely severed—the relationship with a supremely personal God.

The good news is that the help has come. God has intervened in history and reconciled humanity to Himself through Jesus Christ (2 Corinthians 5:18–21). The relationship and the fellowship between us and God can be restored when we confess our need for help and place our faith in the atoning work of Jesus Christ. As Beth realized, the real issue is not our "enoughness," but Jesus Christ's "enoughness." If the good news of Jesus Christ were posted in a store window, it would say: "Jesus Christ can make the world better—if we just confess Him."

11

THE WAY TO NEW LIFE: TRANSFORMATION OR RENEWAL

Art Lindsley

Change is everywhere. Seasons change. Seashores change. Houses get older. Cars rust. Kids grow up. The first sign of gray hair may produce panic. It is not always easy to decide whether change is good or bad, but one thing is certain: Change goes on, whether we like it or not.

The ancient Greeks debated the nature of change. Heracleitus maintained that change was all there was: All is becoming; everything is in flux. Parmenides, on the other hand, held that whatever is—is. As well as that which changes, there is that which does not change. As well as becoming, there is being.

This debate is still with us. Today the New Age movement sides with Heracleitus and believes all is becoming and that which we see has no real being.

The New Age movement uses the word *transformation* as one of its key words. Two books argue for this "new age" form of transformation: Marilyn Ferguson's *The Aquarian Conspiracy* and George B. Leonard's *The Transformation*. Both books are manifestos for a radically altered consciousness. Both attempt to summarize a basic unity behind what, on the surface, may seem to be a widely diverse movement. They maintain that all, indeed, is one—and that we need to look beyond appearances (illusion) and perceive the unity of all things. They suggest a variety of methods to alter our consciousness and acquire unlimited power over the world. Both books call for a personal and social transformation, a transformation which is completely different from the Christian view.

Although the New Age movement has its American roots in the sixties and seventies, it has only recently come to the attention of many Christians. Harvey Cox documented this movement in the seventies in *Turning East*. Later controversial best-sellers such as Constance Cumbey's *The Hidden Dangers of the Rainbow* and Dave Hunt's *Peace, Prosperity and the Coming Holocaust* made the New Age movement a new issue for many people. Both of these authors were alarmed at the dangers of the New Age movement and viewed it in the context of end-times prophecy. However, neither analyzed the assumptions of the New Age movement or its views on personal and social transformation.

Unfortunately, while Christians have been recently more critical of the cultural *isms*, they have neglected to offer a positive view of personal and social transformation. Perhaps a need to answer the attacks of a post-Christian culture has provoked this defensive posture, but we must beware. It is often said that "cults are the unpaid bills of the Church." At the same time, the New Age program exposes areas that Christians have inadequately examined—part of the appeal of Ferguson's and Leonard's books is the "holistic" scope of their works. To argue against the New Age alternative, Christians should include thorough studies of the Christian perspective on consciousness, reason, intuition, human potential, education, politics, vocation, ecology, and other areas.

Although the New Age movement provides a comprehensive view of transformation, its assumptions cannot support that view. Fundamental inconsistencies in their view undercut the New Age program of personal and social transformation.

This chapter will contrast New Age and biblical views of transformation. We will examine such questions as: *What* is the nature of the reality that is to be transformed? *Why* does it need to be changed? *How* do you change it? *When* will the change be accomplished?

The New Age View of Reality

What is the nature of the reality that must be transformed? The New Age view maintains that God and the world are the same reality. Therefore, the nature of reality is divine. On the one hand, God is a principle, a universal law, a vibration, an energy, or a cosmic consciousness; on the other hand, human beings are a part or a mode of God. In other words, "All is one and all is God."

Though some classical traditions of Hinduism teach this pantheistic worldview, the New Age movement alters it slightly, to make it more palatable to the Western scientific mind. New Age works are filled with allusions to Western scientific research on physics, medicine, the body-mind relationship, and psychology, which are used to argue that reality is not as it appears. Nevertheless, although their concepts are clothed in Western scientific and literary style, they clearly teach the pantheistic worldview.

Marilyn Ferguson (1980, 100) maintains that the "separate self is an illusion" and that reality consists of an "even larger Self." Any appearance of separateness or distinction in reality is an illusion. Ferguson holds to the principle of nondistinction, which means everything is interconnected. The concreteness of the world is illusion (180). Moreover, the principle of nondistinction proclaims that humanity is one with everything (172).

George Leonard (1972) also maintains that the first step in the transformation is a sense of oneness with all existence, and the distinctions we make are caused by a false perception of reality. This sense of oneness can occur spontaneously while we are out in the sun or playing music. It "summons us to dismantle the walls between ourselves and our sisters and brothers, to dissolve the distinctions between flesh and spirit, to transcend the present limit of time and matter" (236).

The Christian View of Reality

The Christian view of reality starts with the concept of creation. Numerous biblical passages affirm the basic distinction between God the Creator and His creation (Isaiah 40:29–31; 44:22–26; Psalms 90:1–2; 89:11–15; 139; 147; 148; John 1:1; Revelation 1:11; 4:8, 11). Moreover, Christians historically have affirmed that this creation is *ex nihilo*–out of nothing. This implies a denial of the dualism of the Greeks and pantheism. Against dualism, the Christian affirms that God is the Creator of everything, including matter, and that matter is good, not evil. Against pantheism, the Christian affirms that matter is real, not illusory. Therefore, creation is both good and real.

New Age Problems With Reality

To New Agers, this world is a shadowy world of unreality. It is the realm of illusion, produced by our inability to see unity behind the diversity (Gilkey 1959, 59–61). Pantheism has normally led to an escape from concrete existence, into a life of meditation and isolation. Thus, in its most consistent and pure form, pantheism has not provided an impetus for social change or scientific research. Social transformation would amount to reorganizing illusion. Scientific research would amount to systematizing illusion. Therein lies the basic contradiction within the New Age movement: Their philosophy undermines the scientific evidence they use to argue their view.

Ferguson, Leonard, and others from the New Age perspective make a prodigious effort to provide scientific evidence to support their program for personal and social transformation. Yet their assumptions are inconsistent with the methods of science. While science deals with the interrelationships of causes, the New Age movement denies the reality of causality (Ferguson 1980, 106). While science deals with classifications and distinctions, the New Age movement holds to the principle of nondistinction. They totally undermine the motive, methodology, and validity of science.

Many scholars have recognized that it is only under the Christian doctrine of creation that science has flourished (Ramm 1972; Barbour 1966). Because the finite world is real and good, it should be studied. Because God is an all-wise Creator, there is an order to the world that can be discerned and systematized.

Another problem for New Age proponents is that they call for *personal* transformation, which is inconsistent with their assertions that individual personality is illusory. On the surface, it may seem the New Age idea of identification with God is the supreme compliment. Yet it also means we have no individuality. The distinction between you and me, between you and a tree, between you and God, is unreal. New Agers maintain that the key to fulfillment is an awareness that all distinctions are unreal.

However, if this is true, it leads to a strange conclusion. Since human beings do not have a distinct nature, we can only be fulfilled as individuals by realizing our nonindividuality. We must think ourselves out of concrete existence. We can only fulfill ourselves by realizing that we are not ourselves, but part of the "Self." The way to personal transformation is the death of personality.

The Christian view of creation provides the basis for real personal transformation. God has created persons in His own image. Each person has his or her own being, character, personality, and gifts. Individuality is good. Each person has unique potential, value, and creativity. Gilkey (1959, 62) says:

> ... individual concrete existence is not an evil thing that is to be progressively lost in religion; it is an essentially and potentially good thing that can be recreated. Creatures are, in Christian eyes, entities capable under God of experiencing and embodying value, for despite their contingency and temporality, each creature has the possibility of the genuine fulfillment of its nature ... This Christian conception of creation as the establishment of a real world of potential, even if as yet unrealized goodness, has had a tremendous influence on our Western culture.

Only when we see the New Age movement's implicit denial of the reality and goodness of individual personality do we clearly see the tremendous benefits of the Christian doctrine of creation.

Spokespeople in the New Age movement must resolve one other major problem of their belief system. Not only does the pantheistic perspective undermine the possibility of real personal transformation and individual human potential, it also tends to work against social transformation. Because society has many concrete needs, it is essential to social transformation that its basic structures be real. The New Age movement, however, speaks of concreteness as an illusion. In order to meet the needs of society, it is necessary to distinguish between many complex social needs. Yet, the New Age movement holds to the principle of nondistinction. If all is one, all individual social problems must be illusory.

New Age leaders put forward a program for social transformation, but it is difficult for them to resolve this basic contradiction: How can the principle of nondistinction be *consistently* applied to the complexities of social needs? The only *consistent* answer is to ignore them—for they do not really exist.

In the Christian view of creation, real value is given to individuals and society. Historically, Christians have been at the forefront of meeting human needs in society. Christians have founded hospitals, worked for the abolition of slavery, provided food, shelter, and comfort.

The basic motive for developing the potential of the individual and society is seen in the "cultural mandate" of Genesis 1:26–28. People made in the image of God are given the task of ruling over all living creatures. They are called to fill and subdue the earth. Certainly, there have been many distortions of this dominion over the earth. These distortions have been due to selfishness, greed, pride, and abuse of power. However, even the acknowledgment of these distortions implies stewardship over creation. We are called to develop the potential of creation for the good of people in society. This assumption is fundamental to the Christian view of vocation and social transformation.

Why Transformation?

Why does there need to be a transformation? Why not be satisfied with the way things are? The New Age answer to these questions is, of course, illusion. We are ignorant of the true nature of reality, they say. Since we lack awareness of the unity of existence, we are deceived by appearances. According to the New Age movement, the problem is that we fail to recognize that what we see is illusion.

For Leonard (1972, 228, 238), the awareness of the oneness of all things *is* the transformation, and lack of this awareness is the problem. We are somehow "marooned between two states of consciousness," (62)—ordinary consciousness and vibrant awareness. Civilization is responsible for this lack of awareness. Though there has been organizational development, there has been "no such development in human consciousness." In other words, since civilization has caused us to perceive the world in a particular way, we need to alter this mode of consciousness to perceive the world correctly.

Ferguson (1980, 376) also argues that the problem is one of "contradictory states of consciousness." Our usual state of consciousness fails to give us accurate knowledge of reality. Only people who enter into other states of consciousness gain accurate information about the universe. Modern research on the brain has shown that "awareness is wider and deeper than anyone had guessed"(154). By the use of psychotechnologies such as sensory deprivation, meditation, and many other means, altered states of consciousness can be explored. In these altered states, "fluctuations may reach a critical level, large enough to provoke a shift into a higher pattern of organization" (168–169). Through altering normal consciousness, we can eliminate illusion and know the oneness of all things.

What Does Christianity Say?

Christianity says the problem is evil, or sin. In many other philosophies, evil is either a necessary part of reality or inherent within creation. For instance, in dualism, evil arises from matter, and only by escaping material reality can evil be eliminated. In naturalism, evil arises from the blind working of natural forces, with disease, earthquakes, and hurricanes being an inevitable part of nature. In pantheism, evil arises from ignorance and individuality. Meanwhile, in Christianity, this evil is neither an original part of God's creation nor a necessary part of the structure of things. There was a time when creation was free of evil; there will be a time in the future when creation will again be free of evil.

As a result of human sin, evil is present in the world. Evil is more than a mere appearance or illusion. Evil is so real that God sent His Son to deal with it on the cross. Christians cannot deny or minimize evil. It is fatal to the Gospel to suppose that evil is unreal or somehow not so bad.

The biblical words for sin present a many-sided picture of evil. Sin bends and distorts the good. Evil breaks up and destroys. Evil is characterized by a rebellious attitude of revolt against God. The biblical words represent sin as confusion, unfaithfulness, vanity, missing the mark, lawlessness, and disobedience (Adams 1979, 147–152). Although evil is a powerful force, it does not have its existence apart from good. Sin is a parasite on the good creation. God can and will eliminate evil from His creation.

New Age Problems With Evil

Since Christianity maintains that evil is not a necessary part of creation, it has had the intellectual problem of dealing with its origin. Why is there evil, if God is all-powerful and good? Because the New Age movement has identified finitude with evil, it does not have the same intellectual problem with evil. However, the New Age's unfortunate conclusion is that the only way to eliminate evil is to eliminate everything finite. Gilkey (1959, 183) explains:

> Evil progressively disappears as finitude disappears; the individual burdens of sin and suffering vanish to the extent that his concern for his own individual finite experience vanishes. The presence of evil in finite experience is rationally explained because finite experience in itself is evil, a "fall" from the unity and harmony of the One. But for the same reason, no redemption of the creature is possible, for creaturehood and suffering are understood to appear and disappear together.

Thus, for the New Age movement, the only way to transform this evil situation is to eliminate the illusion of the finite, the personal, and the social. Disease and suffering are illusory—a matter of consciousness. If we alter consciousness, we eliminate disease. In a chapter entitled "Healing Ourselves," Ferguson cites evidence on the relationship of mind to health. A quote that begins the chapter says, "Complete health and awakening are really the same" (241). Near the end of the chapter, Ferguson says, "We can have it as we imagine and as we will" (277).

A major unanswered question is: How do you account for the reality of the illusion? Why does the illusion of pain and suffering seem so real to us? Why is this illusion universal? There has also been a tendency for pantheism to lack compassion for suffering people. If they are consistent why should they bother with illusory individuals suffering from illusory ailments?

In contrast, the way of Christ is that of compassion for those who are suffering and broken. The Bible says of Christ, in Matthew 12:18–20: "He will proclaim justice to the nations. He will not quarrel or cry out; no one will hear his voice in the streets. A bruised reed he will not break, and a smoldering wick he will not snuff out, till he leads justice to victory." Christ's way of proclaiming justice involves compassion for the weak and oppressed.

The contrast is clear. For the New Age movement, suffering and individuality are part of the illusion, and are to be eliminated together. For the Christian, suffering demands compassion. That compassion is to be continued until He leads justice to victory.

How Can It Be Done?

How can reality be transformed? The New Age solution is to alter consciousness. We can do this by questioning our assumptions and using various techniques to create these altered states of consciousness.

Leonard (1972, 135–139) enumerates some "myths" that must be eliminated if there is to be a new consciousness. In his discussion, we see how far-reaching is the attack on individuality. Some of the myths that Leonard mentions are summarized below.

The myth of separate species. Separating and classifying living organisms is one way of looking at reality. However,

Leonard says that making these distinctions impedes an even more important vision. "In a very real sense there is only one species on this planet and its name is Life on earth."

The myth of the separate ego. In Western civilization, the idea of the separate individual has been greatly emphasized. However, as there has been more contact with Eastern religions, this idea has been eroded. The old way of seeing things still has its advocates, but, according to Leonard, ". . . it is increasingly clear that consciousness has no skin."

The myth of matter, time and space. The idea that matter, time, and space are "discrete and fixed entities is false and misleading."

The myth of illusion. Not only does Leonard maintain that what we think of as real is often actually illusion, but also that what we call illusion may be real. Society has always defined the nature of illusion. Because cultural definitions have limited our human potential to experience the wide range of consciousness, all types of experience should be considered relevant, and none excluded at the start.

The myth of the single body. Leonard believes the physical form of the body is only one of the multiple forms of a human. Hinduism, for instance, talks of five "soul-sheaths." Leonard maintains that this may explain such phenomena as out-of-body experiences.

The myth of old age and death. Leonard foresees a time when "death will have lost its function where human evolution is concerned. Realizing and questioning its utility, we should not be caught by surprise when we find that aging can be greatly slowed or even stopped."

By challenging these and other "myths," New Agers believe our untapped human potential will be released. For example, Leonard describes astral projection as a means of intergalactic travel. He says, "Along with jet and rocket flight we can seek to fly, as Edgar Mitchell and Charles Lindberg have suggested, by means of something akin to astral projection" (217). Moreover,

Leonard quotes Mitchell as saying that astral projection would be "a lot safer probably than space flight" (172).

New Age transformation is accomplished not only by questioning old assumptions, but also by using "psychotechnologies." These techniques are intended to produce a change in consciousness. Some of the techniques Ferguson (1980, 186–187) mentions are: sensory deprivation or sensory overload (as in the film *Altered States*), biofeedback, hypnosis, meditation, Yoga, karate, rolfing, bioenergetics, and kinesiology. Plus techniques taught in Silva mind control, *est*, Lifespring, Arica, Theosophy, Science of Mind, A Course in Miracles, and Tai Chi.

New Agers say all of these techniques can alter our consciousness, so we are open to a new way of perceiving things. When this is combined with a rigorous challenging of our cultural myths about reality, we can then see the unity of all things.

Transformation starts with the person and moves out into society. However, this New Age transformation proceeds without any binding moral norms. If all is one, and if there are no distinctions in reality, then the distinction between good and evil is unreal. Pointing out this implication in the principle of nondistinction, Ferguson says spiritual traditions holding to this view of reality maintain "there is no good or evil" (381).

Ferguson quotes the example of a young therapist, who, upon seeing that separations and distinctions are unreal, comes to the conclusion: "I see that I am already whole, that there is nothing to overcome. In those moments of emptiness of letting be, of complete contact with another, I know that I am all I can be." The only sin, it seems, is ignorance of wholeness and unity; the only evil is the belief in separation or distinction. There is no basis for guilt in the New Age perspective, because there is no fixed standard by which we can be judged.

Of course, it is difficult, if not impossible, to speak to social issues without making moral judgments. For instance, Ferguson's chapter on politics is entitled "Right Power." Certainly this implies that there is a wrong kind of power. In another section, she sugests that "*in* this wholeness, oddly enough,

237

virtues we might once have sought in vain through moral concepts now come spontaneously." The implication is that if there are "virtues," there must be "vices."

Leonard agrees with this denial of moral values. For example, Leonard is particularly critical of the incest taboo of Western culture. He maintains that it "provides a good example of our blindness and confusion on sexual matters" (199). "A transformed vision," he says, "will take us beyond custom and taboo" (177).

In a section on drug usage, Leonard maintains that although the heavy use of marijuana and other more potent drugs has a dulling, deadening effect, the occasional use of the "mild psychedelic marijuana often appears to enhance perception" (193). Moreover, he says, "The more powerful psychedelic—LSD, psilocybin, mescaline and the like—could conceivably find a limited place in a transformed culture. As in some primitive cultures, these agents might be administered during certain significant ceremonies, rites of passage, to help shake up the perceptions. Such ceremonies would be sanctioned and participated in by family, friends, and other respected members of the community" (193).

In the area of education, Ferguson critiques the old academic (left brain) way of education. She is in favor of an approach that is more creative (right brain), taking into account altered states of consciousness. Ferguson (315) supports a curriculum that takes altered states of consciousness seriously and advocates the use of "centering," meditation, and other exercises that would encourage "whole brain learning."

In the area of vocation, Ferguson calls for a redefinition of security and success. Above all, she calls for people to go-for-it, moving out of conventional jobs into ones corresponding to their dreams and desires. Follow the way that makes you feel better and enhances consciousness; reject that which dulls consciousness, such as repetitive, conventional jobs.

In the area of medicine, she critiques those who fail to take into account the whole person, arguing for holistic health.

Christians would certainly agree with much in Ferguson's

social critique, although for different reasons. Nevertheless, it must be asked if any of these critiques are consistent with the principle of nondistinction. Many distinctions, moral and otherwise, are selectively made. When it is to their advantage, New Age advocates employ Western science, logic, literary style, and morality. When it is not to their advantage, they scream "Western rationalist." Ferguson and Leonard seem to be unaware of the influence of Christian values and assumptions in their use of language, logical distinctions, moral judgments, and social critique.

The Christian Way of Transformation

In two ways, the Christian perspective is like that of the New Age movement: It views transformation as moving from the inside out, and it calls for a transformation of every area of life. However, Christians are not transformed by altering their consciousness, but by the Gospel of Jesus Christ. As our broken relationship with God is restored, we see clearly why we were created. We were created to know God through Christ, to experience fellowship with others, and to develop the potential of our own gifts and that of the creation—all for the glory of God.

Transformation begins with regeneration. We need to be born from above (John 3:1–10). Salvation is by grace alone, through faith alone, by Christ alone. Because the Holy Spirit changes our desires, we want to follow God's commandments. We once loved darkness, but now we love the light (John 3:19–20). We now have a new status: God is our Father (Matthew 6:9) and we are heirs of God and joint heirs with Christ (Romans 8:15–17). God has made us accepted in the Beloved (Ephesians 1:6). Christ is our Advocate. Our bodies are temples of the Holy Spirit (1 Corinthians 6:19). The fruit of the Spirit is evident in our lives (Galatians 5:22). We are new creatures (2 Corinthians 5:17), with a new self (Colossians 4:10; Ephesians 4:24)—a chosen race, a holy nation, a royal priesthood, a member of the people of God (1 Peter 2:9).

Transformation proceeds from the inside out. Regeneration not only gives us new desires, but begins a process by which our old character is changed. Old patterns are altered, old habits defeated: There is a transformation of our character. One of the means by which this transformation is accomplished is through the Word of God, which renews our minds. Paul teaches, "Do not conform any longer to the pattern of this world, but be transformed by the renewing of your mind . . ." (Romans 12:2).

It is by means of preaching, teaching, and studying God's Word that this transformation progresses. The Holy Spirit imprints on our hearts and consciences that which we learn. Therefore, we are to "prepare [our] minds for action" (1 Peter 1:13) and "crave pure spiritual milk, so that by it you may grow up in your salvation" (1 Peter 2:2).

A primary motive for transformation is gratitude. Because of the mercies of God, we offer ourselves as living sacrifices and renew our minds. Our obedience is a response to what God has done. We are not to live our lives in joyless, legalistic obedience, but with hearts "overflowing with thankfulness" (Colossians 2:7). We are to receive all that God has created with gratitude.

Transformation involves the whole creation. Redemption is not only for people, but for all of creation. Paul teaches that creation, which was "subjected to frustration," will be "liberated from its bondage to decay" (Romans 8:20–22). God has begun a process that will not only transform us, but restore everything (Acts 3:21). There will be a new heaven and a new earth (2 Peter 3:13; Revelation 21:1).

Transformation involves all areas of life. We are called to be holy in all our behavior (1 Peter 1:15). We are to reflect holiness in our personal and social lives. No area is exempt from the need for transformation or reformation. We need to recapture some of the passion for reformation held by Christians throughout the ages. For instance, Thomas Case, in the seventeenth century, said (Walzer 1965, 10):

> Reformation must be universal ... reform all
> places, all persons and all callings, reform the
> benches of judgment, the inferior magistrates ...
> Reform the cities, reform the country, reform inferior
> schools of learning, reform the Sabbath, reform the
> ordinances, the worship of God ... you have more to
> do than I can speak.... Every plant which my
> heavenly Father hath not planted must be rooted up.

Although many Christians in the past have held this comprehensive view of reformation or transformation, it is not always emphasized today. Many Christians today are individualistic, stressing personal salvation. While it is important to maintain the primacy of personal salvation and evangelism, it is also important to follow biblical commands to do justice in society. We need to be aware of the subtle and not-so-subtle forms of evil in our society.

It's good to see a number of Christian writers calling for personal *and* social transformation. Books like *Dynamics of Spiritual Life; Idols for Destruction; Until Justice and Peace Embrace; Idols of Our Time,* and *All of Life Redeemed* point out central problems in our society and show a biblical perspective on how to change them. Nevertheless, there needs to be further work on the biblical foundations of personal and social transformation.

Transformation is never completed in this life. An often-used Latin motto says: *Ecclesia reformata est semper reformanda*—a reformed Church is always reforming. Although we can learn from the past, we should not look to the first, sixteenth, or seventeenth centuries for perfection. Unless we are willing to maintain that our traditions are infallible, we must continually evaluate them by Scripture.

We can learn to be reformers from the example of Christ. On the one hand, Christ was not a conservative: He was not afraid to criticize the traditions of His Church and culture. On the other hand, Christ was not revolutionary: He taught some things were worth preserving. For example, He stood on the unchanging Word of God. But Christ also knew that as reformers, we need to be continuously reformed. Christ was not a utopian; He was fully aware of the extent of human sin and its effects.

Transformation is for eternity. We are "born again, not of perishable seed, but of imperishable" (1 Peter 1:23). Grass withers, and the flower fades, but God's salvation will last forever. The glory reflected on Moses's face, when he descended from Mount Sinai and the presence of the Lord, faded. However, our glory will never fade away (1 Peter 5:4), and we "are being *transformed* into his likeness with ever-increasing glory" (2 Corinthians 3:18).

When Will Transformation Take Place?

When will the transformation be accomplished? What is the basis for our hoping that this change will be achieved? The New Age perspective maintains there is no real difference between past and future; time and history are both part of the illusion. Christians claim there will come a decisive moment in history when God will judge evil. Thereafter, His people will relate to Him for all eternity.

Ferguson and Leonard often speak of a coming New Age, when there will be a "new mind." They believe that this New Age is coming. The future is spoken of in utopian language. Optimism radiates throughout their books. We need to ask whether their appeal to a coming New Age (with its implied contrast to an old age) and their hope for the future are consistent with their basic assumptions, since, despite their language, New Agers still deny the reality of historical time.

Leonard argues that the sense of oneness he desires is distinct from the idea of time. When consciousness is altered, we see that all time is identical. Leonard (1972, 61) says:

> . . . time must be set off as a separate category from the vibrancy. For us, time is a matrix against which pulsation and pattern reveal themselves. To place

time in the same category with the vibrancy is to take a further leap of conceptualization and being. It is perhaps to enter the highest mystical state, the *nirvikalpa samadhi* of the Hindus, in which case all things are experienced as identical, eternal, and ecstatic.

Notice the last phrase. In an altered state of consciousness, all things are identical and eternal. In other words, they are not distinct and temporal. The freedom of the transformation is that "we may choose to alter time" (175) or "transcend the present limits of time and matter" (236).

Leonard suggests that all the perceived tides of history, the great leaps forward, are illusion (120). In yet another passage, he quotes a Zen philosopher who maintains: "Nighttime and daytime are not different. The same thing is sometimes called nighttime, sometimes called daytime. They are one thing" (119). Once we transcend the limited way we perceive time, the world becomes literally different (121).

Ferguson also maintains that our culture has distorted our view of time and reality is not what it appears. There is no space, no time—just events. We are captives of our cultural idea of time, which is "monochronic"—linear, like a road or ribbon extending back into the past and forward into the future (Ferguson 1980, 104). This is contrasted with "polychronic" time, which is nonlinear.

This challenge to the existence and nature of time may seem to be novel, but it has a long history. Numerous cultures, including India and ancient Greece, have held a cyclical view of time and history. A cyclical view of time denies that history has a goal: Nothing is really new, nothing will endure. In Hinduism, these cycles have various applications, but usually they involve the transmigration of souls (reincarnation)—seemingly endless cycles that lead to an eventual absorption into the oneness of being. Once this goal is attained, the whole cycle will be repeated again and again. Augustine criticized this view of time (Gilkey 1959, 248):

They have therefore asserted that these cycles will
ceaselessly recur, one passing away and another
coming ... the things which have been, and those
which are to be coinciding. And from this vicissitude
they exempt not even the immortal soul that has
attained wisdom, consigning it a ceaseless transmigration between delusive blessedness and real misery.

In order for life to have any sense of meaning, certain
conditions are necessary. We must have a reason to hope for the
ultimate fulfillment of our deepest human needs. In the midst
of our struggles, we must have a promise of inner health. We
also need a goal that has not yet been achieved and will not
vanish. But both the Indian and Greek cultures (except during
certain optimistic periods) have led to a predominantly negative view of life. Gilkey (159) argues that the pantheistic view of
life tends to lead to a sense of meaninglessness: "Whereas in
the Hellenistic and Indian cultures life was essentially meaningless because finitude and evil were identified, in Christian
faith life is potentially meaningful because finite existence is
essentially good rather than evil."

According to the New Age movement, life—as we experience
it—is an illusion. Personality and society are an illusion. As
long as we remain individuals, we can never meet our deepest
needs; and because we cannot escape this illusion for very
long, most of our lives will be lived in frustration. Although we
may experience moments of oneness, we cannot have inner
health as long as the illusion persists. Gilkey (248) argues:

> One of the most significant and dramatic turning
> points in the development of Western culture was
> the victory over this deadly view of circular time
> achieved by the biblical view of history. As impor-
> tant, culturally, as the destruction of the pagan gods
> was the overthrowing of endless cycles.... The
> contrast between these two conceptions is absolute;

and only a faith as virile and certain as that of early Christianity could have uprooted the ingrained sense of temporal meaninglessness that permeated and deadened the ancient world.

Although the New Age movement is extremely optimistic about the coming of a New Age, what is the basis for its hope? It seems to be a bare assertion. If there is no real future, how can we be optimistic about it? If there is no time, how can there be a New Age?

Time and Eternity

The biblical view of history is that time has a beginning and history is moving in a direction controlled by God. Both time and history are significant. We are to number our days (see Psalms 90:12), that we might gain a heart of wisdom. We are to redeem the time (see Ephesians 5:16) that we do have.

Christians affirm that history is significant. There are in history new, irreversible, and eternally significant events— salvation is manifested in history. Moreover, moments of time derive their significance and meaning because they lead toward an eternal goal.

The biblical view of history restores meaning to events that would otherwise be without significance. Since God governs history, Christians can be optimistic about the future. Almost any amount of suffering and deprivation can be accepted when it is viewed as part of an intelligible order moving toward a goal (Romans 8:28).

Christians can be optimistic because the victory over evil has been won on the cross. Moreover, the Christian hope for eternal salvation in God's heavenly kingdom is a sure and steadfast anchor for our souls (Hebrews 6:19). Our hope is not uncertain because we have a solid basis for that hope. Our God is a God of hope; our certainty lies in the character of God.

Since we understand the importance and significance of time, we see there is a relationship between what we do now and the future: Actions have consequences. Nothing that we do for the Lord is in vain (*see* 1 Corinthians 15:58).

Since the New Age movement denies the ultimate reality of history and time, it fails to justify their hope for a better future. Since there is no real future, their hope for personal and social transformation is as illusory as their view of personality and society.

The biblical view sets forth a positive basis for personality and society. Transformation leads to personal and social wholeness. Amidst the struggles of the present, we know the outcome of history. We have previewed the final act. Our God is the basis for our certainty that personal and social transformation will happen.

Appendix
NEW AGE AND BIBLICAL WORLD VIEWS

Brooks Alexander and Robert Burrows

THIS CHART IS INTENDED TO ILLUSTRATE THE DIFFERENCE BETWEEN NEW Age and biblical worldviews. It is also arranged to illustrate the internal logic and coherency of the worldviews themselves.

Virgil correctly said, "We make our destinies by our choice of gods." Our conception of God, the divine, or ultimate reality, determines the rest of our worldview; and that worldview is fleshed out in our lives. We are shaped by who or what we worship. When God is conceived as impersonal, amoral energy, humanity is similarly conceived. When God is conceived as personal, caring, and moral, so, too, is humankind. If we do not see God clearly, we will see nothing clearly, including ourselves.

NEW AGE WORLD VIEW/BIBLICAL WORLD VIEW

God

1. Ultimate reality (god) is one and impersonal. Being one, it contains no distinctions, is undifferentiated, without qualities or attributes. It thus unifies all dualities and transcends all values, including good and evil. It cannot be personal, since personality is a by-product of differentiation and distinction. It therefore has no will and harbors no purposes. God is pure unmanifest energy, and the cosmos is the permutations of that energy, according to strict laws of cause and effect.

1. God is personal and has attributes appropriate to personality: will, purpose, values, concerns, freedom, creativity, and responsiveness. These attributes are reflected in all that God is and does. All of God's creation portrays some features of His nature, but the highest aspect of His being—personality—is specifically displayed by the highest development of His creation: humankind.

God and Creation

2. God emanates the cosmos out of its own being. The cosmos therefore is an extension of god, has the nature of god, and, in essence, is god. There ultimately is no distinction or discontinuity between god and the cosmos: *All is one.* God is creation.

2. God creates the cosmos out of nothing. God transcends His creation and is distinct from it. There is a radical discontinuity between God and what He has made. The cosmos is not God and does not share His essential being. It is subordinate to God, and God is sovereign over it. God is not creation.

248

3. The emanations of god—the cosmos—are appearances which have only a limited and deceptive reality. The full reality behind all appearances is the one, which does not allow particularity of existence in any form, by definition. The cosmos is therefore *maya*—the play of illusion. It has a largely negative value insofar as we take it for real.

3. The creation is both real and good. When God created *ex nihilo*—out of nothing—He brought a genuine novelty into existence. It was neither God nor nothing, but something. The creation is now flawed and fallen. Even so, it continues to display the imprint of its Creator and remains in God's sight "very good." In the end, God will renew it, not reject it.

Humanity

4. Humanity also is not distinct from god. Human beings, like the rest of the cosmos, are in essence made out of god. Like ultimate reality, they are reducible to pure consciousness, featureless and impersonal.

Thus, humanity, too, has no definite nature. Whatever nature it seems to have is illusory.

5. Human beings, therefore, like ultimate reality, have no innate attributes or inherent limitations. No particular values or functions come as a given of the human condition. Human nature is not fixed in any regard, but is protean and infinitely flexi-

4. Humanity is part of creation. We share its reality and goodness. Human beings are constructed to provide for the growth and development of personhood, precisely because God Himself is personal. God purposely conducted the course of creation toward the pinnacle of personhood.

5. Human beings, therefore, have a particular design, which yet provides for individual development. The limitations of finite existence are not chains of the spirit; they are boundaries which provide for the play of freedom. The particularities and

ble. All options are open. Humanity therefore has infinite potential. Human beings inherently embody all the power, knowledge, and wisdom of the cosmos, as well as its divine nature. Humanity is god.

6. Divine humanity has no limits and confronts no unbreachable barriers. Mortality is unreal. Death is the final stage of growth; it resembles termination only from the viewpoint of the illusory, separate self. Death is a process within the illusory cosmos and is therefore an illusion as well. The impersonal ground of existence is deathless and unchanging. Human beings, in their divine essence, are therefore immortal. Ultimately, death does not exist.

limitations of created existence are intended, designed, and blessed by God. This also means that human beings are distinct from God and subject to Him. No created thing can bear the burden of divinity. Humanity is not God.

6. In addition to the providential boundaries of created existence, there are further limits introduced by the brokenness of sin. Many of the limits we experience are the result of the curse that followed the Fall (Genesis 3:14–19). Death in particular, the predicted destroyer, raises a baffling barrier to the human quest for meaning. Death reduces our limited life to meaningless absurdity. Because its reign is universal, it nullifies hope and achievement. Death is God's judgment on sin and is therefore real and inescapable.

Humanity's Link With God

7. Humanity's link with ultimate reality is based on the oneness of all existence and its essential unity with the divine. There may be self-imposed barriers to the per-

7. Humanity's connection with God is through communion in relationship. The distinction between God and His creation permits an appropriate and fulfilling relat-

ception of this unity, but there is no discontinuity of being at any point.

edness. God created us for this purpose, and He endowed us with person-hood—His image—to this end.

Humanity's Dilemma

8. The dilemma of humanity is a constriction of awareness.
We have limited our con-sciousness so we do not per-ceive the one, but only fragments of it. Our problem is metaphysical ignorance.

8. The dilemma of humanity is a broken relationship with the God of creation. Our pri-mal ancestors were dismissed from the presence of God—in part for their own protection. All their descen-dants are likewise born into spiritual exile. We have made ourselves enemies of God. We have lost the very relationship in which we were designed to find fulfillment.

9. The limitations on our awareness are imposed by various forms of social condi-tioning. From the beginning, we are taught to break reality up into parts and pieces: good and bad, us and them, me and you, etc. As we move into adulthood, these mental systems become more sophis-ticated, but no less divisive. Self, family, nation, race, and "matter" all define illusory boundaries where there is only oneness.

9. The source of our loss of relationship with God is hu-man rebellion, ancient and enduring. Rebellion, freely willed, has poisoned our gene-pool. It is both our in-heritance and our tradition. Our inborn and inbred re-sponse to God is rejection: struggle or evasion, fight or flight. We continually turn our backs on God, not just with indifference, but with hostility. The career of Jesus clearly demonstrates that if

Reason and belief, in particular, are barriers to a true perception of the one. The fragmenting abstractions of the intellect must be erased and belief-systems that predefine reality must be swept away. Those who preach the primacy of reason or belief obstruct the evolution of humanity and hinder the advent of the New Age.

10. When we see reality in pieces, the effects are numerous and negative.

Subjectively we experience the anxiety and alienation of illusory separateness. Division, hostility, and conflict emerge as alienation is projected onto other, equally illusory "selves," thus deepening and multiplying the mistake. All the hatreds and miseries we see around us derive from the simple error of attributing reality to separate, limited, individual existence.

God plants Himself lovingly in our midst, we will resort to murder to remove Him. That is who we are. We are caught in a situation of our own making which we are powerless to unmake.

10. The nature of sin is rebellion. Its primal and dominating effect is death—an unnatural undoing of the integrity of life. Sin fragments, separates, and alienates. It divides us from God and deepens our spiritual blindness. We begin by rejecting God's presence; we end by denying His reality. Continually avoiding God, we soon cannot see Him at all. Sin also divides people, internally, against themselves. And, of course, it divides human beings against one another. It is useless to talk of humanity solving its own problems as long as it is infected with sin; for it is sin's nature to divide people and turn them against one another.

The Remedy

11. The remedy for our dilemma is to attain knowledge of divine reality—the one. Such knowledge is widely known and goes by many names—*gnosis, enlightenment, god-consciousness.* Whatever it is called, it represents a return to the source, union of dualities, fusion with the one, and transcendence of human nature to self-divinity.

11. The healing of our condition depends on the restoration of our broken relationship with our Creator. There are no techniques to apply, no procedures to learn. As the dilemma is personal and relational, so is its resolution. Healing is initiated by the choice of God and is accepted by the choice of human beings. On the human side, acceptance of God's forgiveness is a turning or revolution. This turning is called "repentance," or *metanoia.* Repentance is simply acknowledgment of what was previously ignored: our creatureliness and dependence on God, but especially our rebellion and hostility against God.

12. The self is both the subject and the agent of enlightenment. Self-realization, as enlightenment is sometimes known, is precisely that—knowledge of the self by the self. Yet the self, as ego or persona, is also the source of the problem. It

12. Repentance is not the source or active factor of salvation. Salvation is a gift. Repentance is the passive act of accepting that gift. The gift is God's reconciling love demonstrated in Christ, who bore our deadly hostility and rose to undo our due

must be undone so the superself—the one—may emerge and be known. Awareness of the one is accessible only to those who can step outside ordinary modes of perception into altered states of consciousness which dispel the illusory boundaries of individual existence. Therefore the self applies to itself techniques of manipulation that finally dissolve its own existence.

If humanity is a cause and effect emanation of the one, the technique of enlightenment is first to control, then to reverse those cause and effects. The process of reversal will be as mechanical and impersonal as the process of manifestation which it seeks to undo—which is to say, totally.

13. The ultimate effect of union with the one is the dissolution of manifest existence in general and of identity and personhood in particular. In effect, enlightenment repeals the curse of life by embracing the curse of death. It undoes the structures of individuation

judgment: death itself. The Gospel is the news of that gift, as an act in space and time.

The entire process of restoration is personal and relational, from its conception in the mind of God to its acceptance or rejection in the minds of humankind.

13. The ultimate effect of salvation is to repeal the curse of death by restoring our relationship with the God of life. When our fundamental relationship is restored, our personhood is properly based and becomes more intense and coherent. The guilt and alienation of

by embracing the powers of disintegration. It ends the alienation of personal existence by ending the existence of the person.

our condition are erased, but the basic structures of individuality are not lost or weakened. The purpose and import of the Gospel is that the personal in humankind be cleansed, not disposed; restored, not rejected; strengthened, not extinguished.

NOTES

Aagaard, J. 1980. Who is who in gurism. *Up-Date:* 4 (Oct.).

Adams, J. 1979. *More than redemption.* Nutley, NJ: Presbyterian and Reformed Publishing.

Anderson, W. 1979. *Open secrets.* New York: Penguin Books.

Aronson, D. 1983. Interview with Sir George Trevelyan. *The New Age Book Review:* 2 (1).

Association for Humanistic Psychology Newsletter. 1975 (Dec.). Review of the film *Where all things belong.*

Baba, M. 1976. *Life at its best.* New York: E. P. Dutton.

Bandow, D. 1984. The U.N. goes for the moon . . . antarctica and the ocean floor. *Inquiry.*

Barbour, I. 1971. *Issues in science and religion.* New York: Harper and Row.

Bartley, W. W. 1978. *Werner Erhard: the transformation of a man: the founding of est.* New York: Clarkson N. Potter.

Blundell, G. 1979. Meditation. In *A visual encyclopedia of unconventional medicine.* A. Hill, ed. New York: Crown.

Bry, A. 1975. *60 hours that transform your life*. New York: Harper and Row.

Bube, A. 1982. Science and pseudoscience. *The Reformed Journal*: 32 (Nov.).

Capra, F. 1975. *The Tao of physics*. Berkeley: Shambhala.

———. 1982. *The turning point*. New York: Simon and Schuster.

Capra, F., and C. Spretnak. 1984. *Green politics*. New York: Dutton.

———. 1984. Who are the greens? *New Age Journal* (Apr.).

Castaneda, C. 1969. *The teachings of Don Juan*. Berkeley: University of California Press.

Chadwick, H. 1955. All things to all men. In M. Black, ed. *New Testament studies*: 1. Cambridge: University Press.

Channon, J. 1982. *Evolutionary tactics*. Privately printed.

Chesterton, G. 1955. *The everlasting man*. New York: Image Books.

Coleman, K. 1979. Elisabeth Kübler-Ross in the afterworld of entities. *New West* (30 July).

Cole-Whittaker, T. 1983. *How to have more in a have-not world*. New York: Fawcett Crest.

Common Ground. 1986. Resources for personal transformation. (Winter).

Coulson, C. 1955. *Science and Christian belief*. Chapel Hill, NC: The University of North Carolina Press.

Creme, B. 1980. *The reappearance of the Christ and the masters of wisdom*. London: Tara Press.

Cumbey, C. 1983. *The hidden dangers of the rainbow*. Shreveport, LA: Huntington House.

Davies, P. 1983. *God and the new physics*. New York: Simon and Schuster.

Deikman, A. 1972. The meaning of everything. *AHP Newsletter* (Apr.).

Dietrich, B. 1987. The coming of a new age. *Seattle Times* (18 Jan.).

Douglas, N., and P. Slinger. 1970. *Sexual secrets.* New York: Destiny Books.

Eliade, M. 1969. *Yoga.* Princeton, NJ: Princeton University Press.

Evans, R. 1975. *Carl Rogers.* New York: Dutton.

Ferguson, M. 1980. *The aquarian conspiracy.* Los Angeles: J. P. Tarcher.

5th Estate. 1986. *Hyping the hungry.* Canadian Broadcasting Corporation.

Fuentes, H. 1979. Allegations of sexual misconduct, cruelty at ranch stir controversy. *San Diego Union* (2 Sept.).

Gilkey, L. 1959. *Maker of heaven and earth.* New York: Doubleday.

Gilman, R. 1982. *Behind world revolution.* Ann Arbor, MI: Insight Books.

Goodspead, E. 1956. *Famous "biblical" hoaxes.* Grand Rapids, MI: Baker Book House.

Green, M. 1970. *Evangelism in the early church.* Grand Rapids, MI: Eerdmans.

Grof, S. 1981. Letter from the president of the International Transpersonal Association.

Guthmann, E. 1986. A spiritual lift through primitive rites. *San Francisco Examiner Date Book* (25 May).

Hanley, J. (n.d.) *The Lifespring Family News:* 1 (1). Available from Lifespring Corporation, 4340 Redwood Highway, Suite 50, San Rafael, CA 94903.

Heisenberg, W. 1958. *Physics and philosophy.* New York: Harper and Brothers.

Hicks, D., and D. Lewis. 1979. *The Todd phenomenon.* Harrison, AR: New Leaf Press.

Houle, C. 1975. Satan is left-handed. Review of the Association for Humanistic Psychology convention.

Hunt, D. 1983. *Peace, prosperity and the coming holocaust.* Eugene, OR: Harvest House.

Jahoda, M. 1982. Wholes and parts: meaning and mechanism. *Nature.*

Jaynes, J. 1982. Imagery and the bicameral mind. The Power of Imagination: Uses of Imagery in the Healing Arts Conference. San Francisco, CA.

Jung, C. 1961. *Memories, dreams, reflections.* A. Jaffe, ed. New York: Random House.

Keys, D. 1982. *Earth at omega.* Boston: Branden Press.

Kilpatrick, K. 1985. *The emperor's new clothes.* Westchester, IL: Crossway Books.

Klein, J. 1979. Esalen slides off the cliff. *Mother Jones* (Dec.).

Knight, J. 1986. *I am Ramtha.* Portland, OR: Beyond Words Publishing.

Knutsen, S. 1978. The meaning of meditation. In *The holistic health handbook.* E. Baumann, A. Brint, L. Piper, P. Wright, eds. Berkeley: And/Or Press.

Krieger, D. 1979. *The therapeutic touch.* Englewood Cliffs, NJ: Prentice-Hall.

Lasch, C. 1977. The narcissistic personality of our time. *Partisan Review* 1.

———. 1986. The infantile illusion of omnipotence and the modern ideology of science. *New Oxford Review* (Oct.).

Leading Edge Bulletin 1 (no. 1) (1980).

Leading Edge Bulletin 2 (no. 14) (1982).

Leonard, G. 1972. *The transformation.* Los Angeles: J. P. Tarcher.

LeShan, L. 1975. *The medium, the mystic, and the physicist.* New York: Random House.

Lidz, T. 1973. *The origin and treatment of schizophrenic disorders.* New York: Basic Books.

Lilly, J. 1977. *The deep self.* New York: Warner Books.

Loomis, E. 1977. The healing center of the future. *Journal of Holistic Health.*

MacKay, D. 1974. *The clock work image.* Downers Grove, IL: InterVarsity Press.

McRae, R. 1984. *Mind wars.* New York: St. Martin's Press.

Maharishi Mahesh Yogi. 1968. *Meditations of Maharishi Mahesh Yogi.* New York: Bantam Books.

Mangalwadi, V. 1984. How to answer a Hindu. *Cornerstone* (Sept.).

Marin, P. 1975. The new narcissism. *Harpers* (Oct.).

Marsden, G. 1980. *Fundamentalism and American culture.* New York: Oxford University Press.

———. 1982. The new fundamentalism. *The Reformed Journal:* 32 (Feb.).

Maslow, A. 1968. *Toward a psychology of being.* 2d ed. New York: Van Nostrand Reinhold Company.

Masterson, J. 1980. *From borderline adolescent to functioning adult.* New York: Brunner/Mazel.

Masterson, J. F. 1976. *Psychotherapy of the borderline adult: a developmental approach.* New York: Brunner/Mazel.

Masterson, J. F. 1985. *The real self: a developmental, self and object relations approach.* New York: Brunner/Mazel.

Metzger, D. 1985. Revamping the world. Reprinted in the *Utne Reader* (Aug./Sept.).

Mitchell, E. 1983. *Bridging science and metaphysics in the 20th century.* Cassette recording. Del Mar, CA: Mandala Media.

Mookerjee, A., and M. Khanna. 1977. *The tantric way.* Boston: New York Graphic Society.

Moss, R. 1983. Awakening the energies of transformation. Paper presented at the ninth annual Mandala conference.

Muller, R. 1981. *World Goodwill Commentary* (October).

———. 1982. *New genesis.* New York: Doubleday.

Naisbitt, J. 1982. *Megatrends.* New York: Warner Books.

Neibuhr, R. 1953. *Christian realism and world problems.* New York: Scribner.

Pement, E. 1983. Consensus or conspiracy? *Cornerstone:* 11 (64).

Petersen, J. 1982. *Evangelism is a lifestyle.* Colorado Springs, CO: NavPress.

Phelan, N., and M. Volin. 1969. *Sex and Yoga.* New York: Bantam Books.

Rajneesh. 1977. *Come follow me: 2.* Poona, India: Rajneesh Foundation.

———. 1978. *I am the gate.* San Francisco: Perennial.

———. 1984. The center of the cyclone. *The Rajneesh Times* (4 May).

Ramm, B. 1972. *Christian view of science and Scripture.* Downers Grove, IL: InterVarsity Press.

Raschke, C. 1980. *The interruption of eternity.* Chicago: Nelson-Hall.

Renewal. 1980 (8 Sept.).

Renewal. 1982 (31 May).

Rushdoony, R. 1978. *Politics of guilt and pity.* Fairfax, Va.: Thoburn Press.

———. 1979. *Biblical Economics Today* (Oct./Nov.).

Russell, P. 1983. *The global brain.* Los Angeles: J. P. Tarcher.

Satin, M. 1978. *New Age politics.* New York: Delta Books.

Schaeffer, F. 1972. *He is there and he is not silent.* Wheaton, IL: Tyndale.

Simon, A., D. Worthen, and J. Mitas. 1979. An evaluation of iridology. *Journal of the American Medical Association:* 242.

Smilgis, M. 1987. Rock power for health and wealth. *Time* (19 Jan.).

Smith, H. 1979. Consciousness. New Concepts of Consciousness Conference.

Spangler, D. 1977. *Reflections on the Christ.* Scotland: Findhorn.

———. 1980. *Explorations.* Scotland: Findhorn.

Spretnak, C. 1982. *The politics of woman's spirituality.* Garden City, NY: Anchor Books.

Stearn, J. 1976. *The power of alpha-thinking: miracle of the mind.* New York: William Morrow.

Sutphen, S. 1987. Increasing crystal power. *Master of Life.* Malibu, CA: Sutphen Corp.: 33.

Talbot, M. 1981. *Mysticism and the new physics.* New York: Bantam Books.

Tanner, M. 1983. In pursuit of the muse. *GSB* (Spring).

Thompson, W. 1982. *From nations to emanation.* Scotland: Findhorn.

Veith, I., trans. 1966. *Huang ti nei ching su wen (The yellow emperor's classic of internal medicine).* Berkeley: University of California Press.

Viorst, J. 1986. *Necessary losses.* New York: Simon and Schuster.

Vithoulkas, G. 1978. Homeopathy. In *The holistic health handbook.* E. Bauman, A. Brint, L. Piper, P. Wright, eds. Berkeley: And/Or Press.

Walker, B. 1982. *Tantrism.* Wellingborough, Northhampton-shire: Aquarian Press.

Walzer, M. 1965. *The revolution of the saints.* Cambridge, MA: Harvard University Press.

Webb, J. 1976. *The occult establishment.* LaSalle, IL: Open Court Publishing.

Weinberg, S., ed. 1986. *Ramtha.* Eastsound: Sovereignty.

Wilber, K. 1981a. *Up from Eden.* Boulder, CO: Shambhala.

———. 1981b. Republicans, democrats, and mystics. *AHP Newsletter* (Nov.).

———. 1981c. *No boundary.* Boulder, CO: Shambhala.

Zimbardo, P. 1984. Mind control in 1984. *Psychology Today* (Jan.).

Zukav, G. 1979. *The dancing wu li masters.* New York: Morrow.